Making Wood
Folk Instruments

Making Wood Folk Instruments

Dennis Waring

Sterling Publishing Co., Inc.   New York

Acknowledgements

Many people helped me in the preparation of this book. In particular I would like to thank Bev Aronovich who persuaded me of the need for an instruction manual on folk instruments and the Manitoba Arts Council who generously supported my initial research and provided funds for materials to build the models. I am also grateful to Marilyn Malencovik who provided information on the educational use of the instruments I made and to Paul Lewis at the Winnipeg Folklore Center who made available to me a great variety of reference books and records. Walt Lysak helped me put the banjo into perspective and Roldo continuously fed me tidbits of information and let me refer to his extensive instrument collection. Without such interest and help this book would never have been completed.

This book has been published with the aid of a grant from the Manitoba Arts Council.

Note on Metric Conversion

Metric conversion tables for the calculation of instrument measurement are given in Appendix A. No metric measurements have been used in this book, however, because of the difficulty of purchasing some of the needed tools in metric scales. All measurements given are precise and instruments have been built to these specifications. If you wish to substitute metric measurement some experimenting will have to be made with adjusted dimensions before building is started.

Library of Congress Cataloging-in-Publication Data

Waring, Dennis, 1944–
   [Folk instruments]
   Making wood folk instruments / Dennis Waring.
      p.   cm.
   Reprint. Originally published: Folk instruments. Winnipeg : Hyperion Press, c1979.
   1. Musical instruments—Construction.   I. Title.
ML460.W28 1990
784.192′3—dc20   90-37056
                         CIP
                         MN

10 9 8 7 6 5 4 3

Published 1990 by Sterling Publishing Company, Inc.
387 Park Avenue South, New York, N.Y. 10016
Originally published in Canada as *Folk Instruments*
© 1979 by Hyperion Press Limited
Distributed in Canada by Sterling Publishing
% Canadian Manda Group, P.O. Box 920, Station U
Toronto, Ontario, Canada M8Z 5P9
Distributed in Great Britain and Europe by Cassell PLC
Villiers House, 41/47 Strand, London WC2N 5JE, England
Distributed in Australia by Capricorn Ltd.
P.O. Box 665, Lane Cove, NSW 2066
Manufactured in the United States of America

Sterling ISBN 0-8069-7482-6

Table of Contents

Making music is one of the most pleasant and satisfying activities of all life experiences. Sharing music with a friend or a group of people creates, for the music maker, a delight and happiness that transcend most other forms of communication. Even for the solitary performer, music can be a positive avenue of release for inner feelings and emotions. Music's appeal to the senses heightens joy in times of good cheer; its liberating abilities can be cathartic in times of hurt and sorrow. Music is a means of expression that all people understand; it is a language that all people everywhere have in common. No one really knows why music affects us the way it does, but the magic that results from musical experience is undeniable. This book acknowledges the influence and charm of music and proposes that the way to expand the dimensions of music-making pleasure is to build the instrument from which the music will issue.

Musical instruments are an extension of man's body. Just as tools were developed to make arms, hands, and legs more effective, instruments have evolved to extend the capabilities of mouth, vocal chords, and hands in order to express an ever widening variety of sounds. In many cultures, past and present, instruments were important in every aspect of man's life from magic and religion to the deliniation of social structure. Supernatural powers were often attributed to instruments; their influence in both love and war has been documented throughout history.

Access to this special state, however, is not reserved for the highly skilled craftsman and musician. The making and playing of musical instruments can be experienced by anyone who wishes to create his own devices to express himself. The scope of this book provides a variety of building projects and musical experiences that will satisfy both children and adults. Even very young children exhibit an innate interest in sound-making devices. This natural curiosity, if encouraged, can expand the imagination and provide an outlet for youthful energy. The instructions for building the instruments are detailed and easy to follow. Once the basic principles are mastered, however, it's easy to add variations and create your own design. Many children are surprisingly skilled and enjoy contributing their own design ideas and making their own creative decisions. There are many ways to reach the same end and many op-

tions to follow in the choice of materials. In fact, part of the pleasure of the building and playing experience comes through investigating all of these alternatives.

In many countries music makers make use of their immediate environment to provide the means for building their sound-making devices. Gourds, bamboo groves, and vines have great potential in the making of musical instruments. Sometimes these simple instruments play music that is more touching and humanly expressive than all the force of a great symphonic composition. We in North America do not have a ready supply of these natural materials; however, we do have an endless assortment of plastic containers, discarded cans, piping, bottles, and a wide variety of junk that can be recycled into instruments. Any local hardware store and lumberyard can provide the other materials and simple tools that are needed to get the building process underway. The actual construction of a simple instrument is easy but the satisfaction is enormous. Both making and playing provide an outlet for creative energy and players develop skills that extend the range of homemade instruments. In fact, sensitive musicians create highly effective music no matter what sound device they find in their hands.

This book contains building instructions for fifty-one instruments. Detailed diagrams and photographs are included, as well as a listing of required materials. The first section of the book contains guidelines for the making and playing of simple folk instruments which, although not highly sophisticated, are certainly capable of expressing a wide range of meaningful sounds. Often sound effects and tonal explorations discovered through working with simple instruments can lead the builder to try more sophisticated forms. Those who would like to try will find basic directions in the second section of this book. These more complex forms of folk instruments require some specialized tools and hardware, but with some preparation, time, and patience the experience is rewarding. Besides the pleasure it affords, instrument making can be a valuable educational tool for teachers of music, industrial arts, science, and ethnic studies. Instrument making provides "hands-on" experiences whereby children, and adults, can realize their creative and artistic talents.

Our environment is constantly full of auditory impressions we call sounds. Most of these we hear every day and they have become so familiar that we do not think about their origin. Stop and listen. How many different sounds can you count? As we become more aware of individual sounds we are overwhelmed with their incredible variety. High pitched shrieks, low moans, loud crashes, soft whispers are all part of the sound panorama. Some come and leave slowly, others fade quickly; some are pleasant and musical, others are harsh or noisy.

Listen to some of the sounds around you and try to discover the source of each sound. You can hear better if you focus all your attention on the act of hearing. So shut your eyes and let your ears do their work. Now ask yourself what object is producing each sound and what is causing that object to make the sound. There are a great many sound sources that allow you to actually feel and see (as well as hear) the movement that produces the sound. This movement is called "vibration." Some objects, however, vibrate so fast or so slightly that the eye cannot perceive movement except with special devices. The scientific fact is that vibration is the cause of all sound.

Some sounds are classified as "noise" and others as "musical" notes. The best test to differentiate the two is to try to sing the sound to yourself. If you can isolate a singable pitch, it will qualify as a note. The difference between noise and notes is an important piece of physics. Suffice it to say at this point that a musical note has one main vibration in it with a definite number of vibrations per second; whereas, a noise is a jumble of mixed vibrations. Most musical instruments we make will produce definite notes and pitches, although there are a number of percussion instruments that rely on "controlled noise" for their special effect.

What happens after an object is set into vibration?

It then produces sound waves through the air. This effect can be likened to dropping a pebble into a body of water, thus producing a series of concentric waves (A). We should be aware that the air around us has substance; that is to say, it is a nonvisible gas made up of molecules that can be set into motion. Wind is air in motion.

A subtle movement of air molecules occurs when a vibrating object begins a chain reaction among the air particles, causing them to bump against each other in all directions from the vibrating source. It is this reaction among the molecules that is called "sound waves" (B), and they travel at approximately 1100 feet per second (which seems very fast until we think of light traveling at 186,000 *miles* per second). When the sound waves have enough strength to push the ear drum in and out, they are translated into neurological impulses which the brain perceives as sound. The lowest pitch humans can hear is about 20 cps (cycles per second, or sometimes called Hertz); the highest is around 20,000 cps. As we get older, this range may narrow due to "wear and tear" on the ears. It is good practice to always protect your ears from excessively loud sounds and thus preserve hearing sensitivity.

As you probably know, some form of energy is required to set anything moving, which means that energy is required to start the vibrations which result in sounds. The more forceful the energy, the louder the sound. There are several ways to make objects vibrate: the more common types of energy include plucking, blowing, and striking. Bowing and shaking might also be included.

These basic principles of sound will give you some understanding of the scientific basis of how sound is produced. It's time now to turn to the individual instruments described in this book and investigate their sound-making potential.

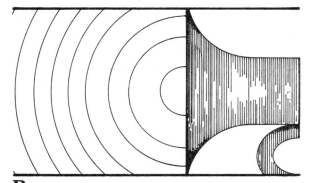

A   **B**

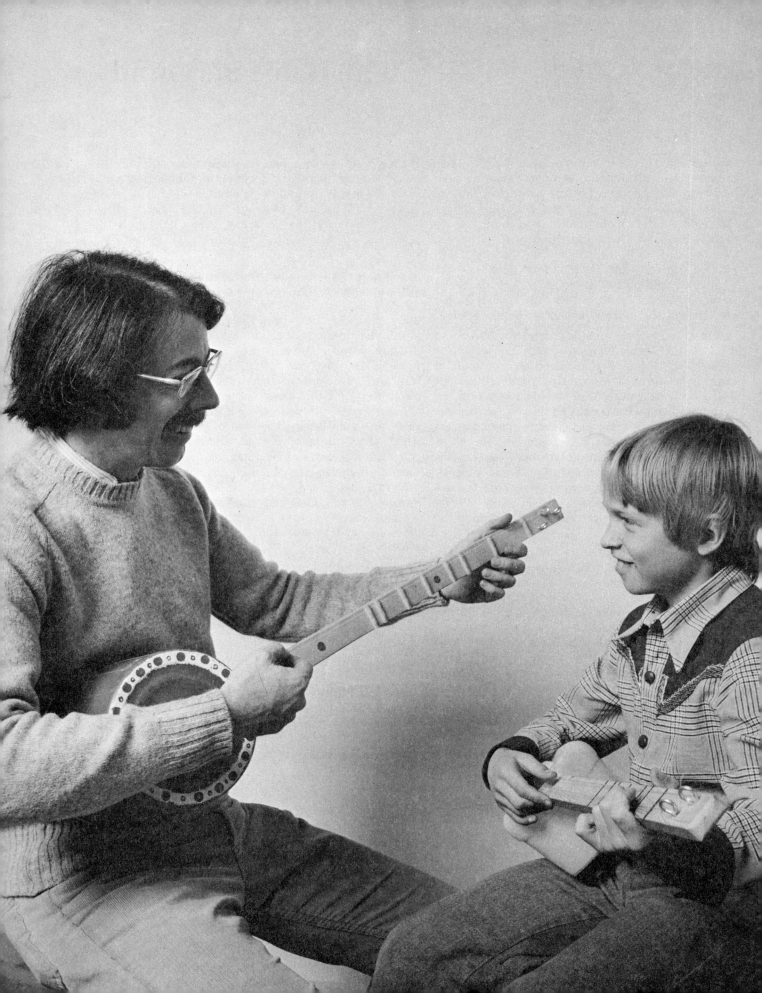

The historical record of most musical instruments is rather sketchy because the perishable materials of which the instruments were made have deprived us of first-hand knowledge of their composition. One of the oldest references, however, has been left in the wall paintings in the caves of Les Trois Frères, and has been dated circa 15,000 B.C. Scholars believe the wall painting depicts a shaman dressed as a bison holding a musical bow against his mouth and performing a dance of enchantment with a real bison (A). From earliest days instruments have been inseparable from ceremonial magic and supernatural ritual. They are still associated with pageants and rites and their power to induce mood change is well known. Another characteristic modern stringed instruments share with their earlier counterparts is that their primary components have remained the same, namely strings and a resonator.

The word "string" is used even though the strings of instruments such as the guitar, piano, harp, and violin are made of steel, nylon, or gut. Silk, twine, and plant fibers have been used in other cultures for the same purpose. How the strings are constructed is important to the kind of sound produced. Some strings are longer than others; some are thicker. Whether strings are tightly stretched or loose also affects their sounds. Consider the following points as a working guide.

These three factors affect the sound.

1. The tension or tightness of the string affects the pitch (the tighter the string, the higher the pitch).
2. The length of the string also affects the pitch (the longer the string, the lower the pitch).

3. The thickness and material of the string affects the pitch and tone quality (the thicker the string, the lower and fuller the sound).

Experiment with different types of strings until you achieve the type of sound desired. You may break a few strings as you try them out, but that is a fairly normal part of the process. However, care must be exercised when fitting an instrument with wire or steel strings. Tensions can reach such a high level that the instrument can literally be pulled apart. If you plan to use steel strings, try to over-build the instrument slightly to compensate for the increased tension.

Strings are activated by *plucking* with the fingers or with plectra made from a quill, bone, or plastic pick (for the guitar). The material used and the style of picking has a great effect on the tone produced. Another widely used method of vibrating strings is *striking* them as with the piano or *bowing* as with the violin. This latter method has been universally adopted, probably because of the voice-like sustained sounds that result.

After the string has been activated, the sound produced is usually amplified, reinforced, and reflected by a hollow chamber to which the strings are attached. Resonators are quite often utilized in their natural form. Gourds, logs, pods, tubes, shells, framed skins, and even human skulls have been used as resonating cavities. Crafted boxes of many shapes and sizes, such as the "waisted" guitar, triangular balalaika, and pear-shaped lute also constitute a large and varied family (B).

Another factor which is of practical concern in the construction of stringed instruments is the tuning mechanism.

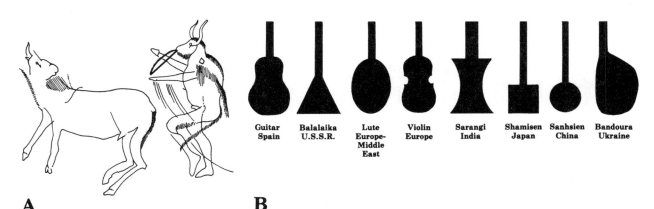

A

B

Guitar Spain — Balalaika U.S.S.R. — Lute Europe-Middle East — Violin Europe — Sarangi India — Shamisen Japan — Sanhsien China — Bandoura Ukraine

Tuning Mechanisms

Tuning mechanisms are one of the most important components on all stringed instruments. The instructions for each of the following instrument projects will focus primarily on a single type of mechanism for the sake of simplicity, but there are a number of options which you should know about from the outset. The design of the instrument may have to be slightly modified if other than the recommended mechanisms are used; however, this should not create a problem if you plan its accommodation beforehand.

SCREW EYES

Probably the simplest mechanisms to regulate the tuning of simple stringed instruments are screw eyes. They should be big enough to turn easily and to hold securely in the wood but small enough so as not to bump into each other during the tuning process. These tuners are easy and inexpensive but are not meant for long-term use because the wood will eventually cease to hold them under tension.

PROCEDURE

1. Use a nail or a drill bit which is slightly smaller than the diameter of the screw eye to start the hole.

2. Start turning the screw eye into the instrument and attach the string with a *good tight knot*. The string should be moderately taut when you attach it so you won't have to turn the screw eye too many times to tighten the string.

3. Screw eyes will turn easier if you put a nail through the eye and use it as a lever (A).

TAPERED DOWELS

Another alternative tuning mechanism which is available at most lumber stores is wooden doweling. Dowels take a little more preparation, but in most cases they look more attractive and provide better stability than screw-eye tuning. If the instrument is to be used over a period of time the wooden dowels will not wear out and slip as quickly as the metal variety.

MATERIALS

1/4" to 1/2" wooden doweling cut into approximately 2" lengths

Drill with a bit slightly smaller than the diameter of the dowel

Note Doweling is often inconsistent in size; usually slightly larger or smaller than advertised, so measure carefully.

1/16" bit for drilling the string hole

Coping, dovetail, or other small saw

Sandpaper

Knife

PROCEDURE

1. Saw doweling into appropriate lengths (2" suggested in most cases).

2. Drill holes into instrument to receive each peg. (It is *always* best to experiment on a scrap piece of wood first to make sure that you have the right combinations and techniques).

3. Whittle and sand one end of each peg to a taper (B) and keep testing peg in peg holes until you get a snug fit. Another option is to saw a 3/8" slot into the end of each peg so that it will compress and hold tension as it is twisted

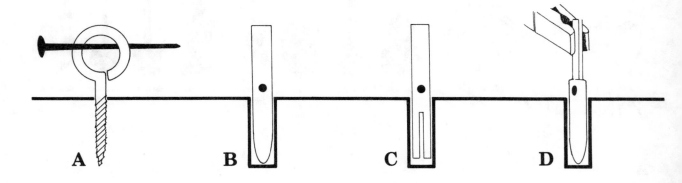

A   B   C   D

into the peg hole (C). You may need a vise to hold the peg as you saw it.

4. To turn the peg, flatten two sides on the end of the peg opposite the tapered or slotted end (D) and use pliers (carefully) or a clothespin fitted to the flattened sides to loosen or tighten the strings. If you use larger tapered dowels you may drill a hole in the end opposite the taper and insert a nail or smaller dowel to give leverage (E).

5. After fitting the peg to the hole, drill a 1/16" hole through the dowel just slightly above the top level of the board.

6. Thread string through hole and tighten.

WOODEN FRICTION PEGS

In addition to metal screw eyes and tapered dowels you can make other tuning mechanisms from a piece of wood that you whittle yourself. Homemade tuners look more authentic and will probably last much longer. These tuners are also called violin pegs and friction pegs. If you wish to use actual violin pegs they can be procured from most music stores.

MATERIALS
A 1" x 3" piece of hardwood for each peg

TOOLS
Coping saw or band saw

Drill with a 3/16" bit and a 1/16" bit

Rat-tail file with 3/16" round

Pocket knife

Sandpaper

PROCEDURE
1. Draw the pattern on each piece of wood (F). Use one peg for each string.

2. Saw away the excess with the saw. If you use a hand saw, it is easier if you clamp the wood down with a small C clamp.

3. Carve the wood until it is tapered and round. The diameter at the small end should not exceed 3/16".

4. Drill a peg hole into the instrument with the 3/16" bit. Make sure holes are spaced evenly so tuners do not collide when turned.

5. Taper the hole with the rat-tail file.

6. Sand the peg until it fits snugly into the hole. (Use soap or peg compound to lubricate the peg for easy turning.) The fit must be accurate or the peg will slip under tension.

7. Put peg in.

8. Mark a dot where the string should go into the peg and drill the string hole with the 1/16" bit (G).

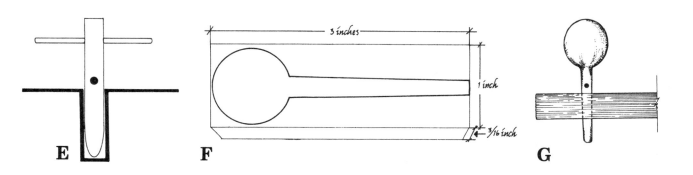

E   F   G

9. Carve the large end of the peg to your liking.

10. Sand the peg.

Now you are ready to string it up.

MACHINE-HEAD TUNERS

Perhaps the most efficient tuning mechanisms are guitar or banjo tuners, although these are more expensive and less authentic than the wooden variety. Machine-head tuners are usually used on more sophisticated instruments and can be purchased at most music stores.

Guitar Tuners are geared so that the string tightens slowly in relationship to the amount of turning. Since there is a wide variety of sizes and styles of machine tuners, you must acquire them early in the building process and construct the peg box accordingly. It is best to inspect a factory-made guitar closely to see how it is fitted. Inspect both classical and steel-string guitars. Some tuners come singly and some come in units of three (these can be sawn apart with a hacksaw if desired).

Two suggestions

1. Make sure the depth of your peg head is thin enough so that the string hole pokes above the top of the board (H).

2. The tiny screws that hold the tuners on may have a tendency to strip or break off unless you predrill a tiny hole slightly smaller than the screw.

Banjo Tuners also come in a variety of styles, sizes, and prices. Some are geared and others work on a squeezing principle which holds the tension of the strings. Again, get the tuners early in the building process, examine factory built banjos to see how the tuners are installed, and do experiments with fitting if necessary before you finalize the design of your own instrument.

ZITHER PINS

Zither pins are used on autoharps, psalteries, hammered dulcimers, harps, and pianos. They are excellent tuning mechanisms for some of the more complex multi-stringed instruments. There are several different sizes and care must be taken (through experimentation or a tried-and-true method that you have used before) to make sure that the peg hole is slightly smaller than the pin so it will not slip under tension. A special key or tuning wrench is necessary to tighten and loosen the strings (I). You may be able to find a clock key to fit the pins. Be sure to get the proper sized key for the pins.

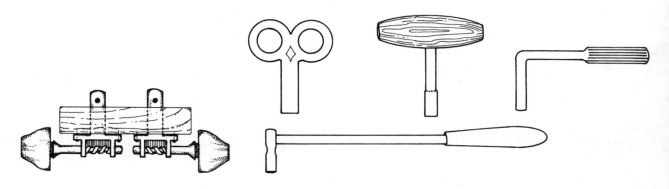

H   I

Although not a genuine instrument, the rubber band harp can reveal much information about acoustical principles and also serve as a fine plaything for younger children. This simple device exemplifies the underlying principle of all stringed instruments. When a vibrating body (the string) is placed onto a resonating chamber which reinforces and enhances the sound (the soundbox), sound results. This basic structure satisfies two of the most important factors involved in making stringed instruments.

Rubber Band Harp

MATERIALS

Several sizes of rubber bands: thin and fat, short and long

Containers such as small-to-medium-sized boxes (match boxes, shoe boxes, cigar boxes, gift boxes, stationery boxes, etc.) and/or wide-mouthed jars

Two pencils or 1/2" dowels that will act as bridges

PROCEDURE

1. Remove the lid from your chosen container and place some rubber bands around it so that they stretch over the opening (A). If they are too loose or too tight, make adjustments with larger or smaller bands. Pluck each band and adjust until it responds with a reasonable "plunk."

2. A clearer pitch may be achieved by placing the pencils under the bands at each end of the box (B). These pencils act as simple "bridges" which determine an exact string length and therefore a more precise pitch. You might also experiment by placing only one pencil under the bands at the center of the box and plucking on either side (C). Move the pencil slightly to one side and you will find an increased range of high and low notes.

3. Steps one and two have involved the rubber bands stretched over an open box. Now try cutting a hole in the center of the box top or lid and replacing it on the box. Add rubber bands and slip pencil "bridges" back under the bands towards the ends of the box (D). The top acts as a simple soundboard and will change the sound characteristics of the box appreciably. By slightly stretching or loosening the rubber bands between the bridges, you may be able to create a simple scale and even compose a short musical piece.

4. Try plucking the bands with a pick. A back and forth strum across all the strings will produce interesting rhythmic effects.

5. Although harder to come upon, small wooden boxes are stronger, will hold up under greater tensions, and will sound a bit more "solid" than their cardboard counterparts.

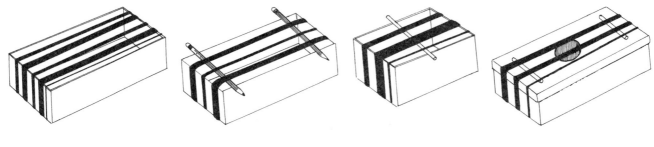

A   **B**   **C**   **D**

Indian Mouth Bow

The mouth bow is perhaps one of the oldest and most universal of all instruments. Wall paintings estimated to be 15,000 years old found in a grotto at Trois Frères in Ariege, France, depict a primitive musical bow. Africans use a bow attached to a gourd for resonance. Inhabitants of the Appalachian Mountains in the United States adopted a bow from the American Indians and use it much like a jaw harp. Its rhythmic and subtle melodic qualities have made it a favorite for accompanying song and dance around the world.

MATERIALS

A tree branch or sapling 3' to 3-1/2' long (longer and shorter bows are also effective), about 3/4" wide on one end and 1/2" wide on the other. Ash, maple, cherry, birch, or other springy hardwood make the best-sounding bows. A yardstick has also been suggested.

One steel guitar string (a 2nd or B string), or high-test nylon fishing line

A light or medium guitar pick

ASSEMBLY

1. Select and cut the branch to the desired length.

2. Trim off leaves and twigs. If you prefer you may peel off the bark, but this is not necessary as long as the branch is clean and smooth, especially at the small end.

3. Cut an angled groove into each end about one inch from the tip (A) or drill a small hole through the branch at each end so the string will go *through* the branch instead of around it (B). If you are using a guitar string you will find a loop or little ring at the end of it. Run the plain end of the guitar string through this ring, forming a loop in the string which will slip around the groove cut in the thin end of the branch (C).

4. Bend the branch into a reasonable curve against the floor with your left hand, while you wrap the loose end of the string several times around the groove at the heavy end.

5. Still holding the bow tense, wrap the string around itself a few times, then back around the groove for a few more turns until it is secure (D).

6. Tuck the rest of the string out of the way and trim off excess.

OPTIONS

1. A worthwhile addition — a resonator — comes from the African form of mouth bow. As discussed previously, an enclosed or semi-enclosed body of air will help to reinforce and enhance the sound of most instruments. Africans achieved greater sound by attaching an open-ended gourd midway on the bow stick (E). A can or plastic jug with one end removed may be used instead of a gourd. Attach it to the bow with a small screw (F). This instrument is often referred to as a gourd bow.

2. A two-note bow can be produced by the addition of a noose which divides the string into two vibrating sections of different pitch (G).

3. A tuning mechanism can also be useful at times to change the fundamental pitch. Drill a hole in the large end of the stick and make a tuning peg for it (H). If you use a yardstick or other

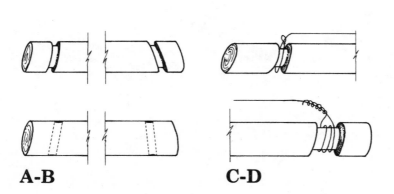

A-B   **C-D**

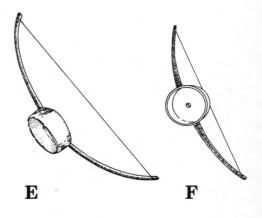

E   **F**

flat-sided stick, a small knob of wood may be glued on one side and a friction peg or guitar tuner attached accordingly (I). Make sure the knob and peg are well secured so they won't spring off under tension.

4. Compound musical bows are an unusual variation on the traditional style of bow. Several strings are attached along different places of a rigid bow-shaped piece of wood (J).

TO PLAY

1. Hold the bow in your left hand (if you are right-handed) about one-third the way down the bow.

2. Place the small end against your right cheek — on the outside of your mouth.

3. Change the pitch by opening your jaws slightly and changing the size of the opening of your mouth. The string will produce one predominant drone, but as you vary your mouth opening you can hear a more subtle pitch change. Control this area to reproduce a melodic line.

4. Hold a fairly thin, large pick in the right hand and strum it back and forth across the string. Get a good grip on the pick and begin slowly to get the feel of it — back and forth, back and forth. Now try to build up speed without losing the steady rhythm. Keep practising. The instrument is also played by tapping the string with a light stick.

Note Different pitches for the drone can be created by slightly bending the bow as you play.

PLAYING SUGGESTIONS

Any song that has a steady beat and a small range may be used. A mouth bow goes especially well with the solo voice. If you are by yourself, you could sing a verse or two, then play the melody on the mouth bow — another verse or two and another break with the bow, etc. Listen to some of the songs of Buffy Ste. Marie and notice the variety and mood she creates with the mouth bow. With a group of music makers, the mouth bow provides a nice rhythmic effect. Play the song with a guitar. The drone note of the bow should be the key note of the song. The string can be tightened by re-looping the string, or use one of the previously mentioned suggestions for tuning pegs. Add rhythm instruments or simply clap along.

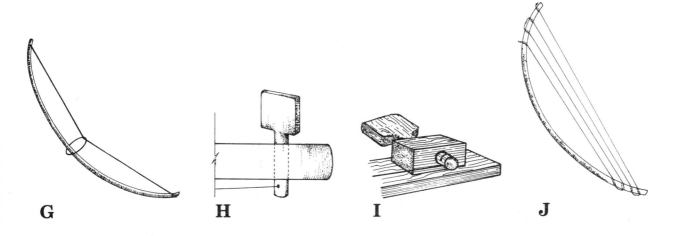

G   **H**   **I**   **J**

Wall Harp

I include this instrument primarily to show the resourcefulness and ingenuity of the musical spirit. The wall harp originated in rural areas of southern United States, where at one time blacks and whites were too poor to own instruments. The wall acts as the sound-box.

MATERIALS

Two large nails

A wire or other string from 3' to 8' long

A stone or piece of wood to act as a bridge

A bottleneck (A) or segment of metal tubing about 3" long (B)

Plectrum

TOOLS

Hammer

PROCEDURE

1. Hammer two nails into the side of a house, barn, garage, or structure preferably with hollow walls.

2. Stretch and secure wire tightly between nails.

3. Jam stone or wood chunk under wire. The wire may be tuned depending upon the placement of this "bridge."

TO PLAY

The "string" should be fairly tight for best tone production. As the string is plucked, strummed, or tapped, slide the bottleneck up and down the string, at times creating slippery glissandos, at other times centering on notes that accompany or create a melody. The wall harp was probably used mostly as accompaniment to blues singing.

A

B

An interesting variation on the bow principle (and the washtub bass) is the ground bow, sometimes called a "pit harp" in Africa or "mosquito drum" in Haiti. The earth makes a very good resonator of sound, giving a deep mellow color to the tone.

MATERIALS

A flexible pole about 6' or 7' long

4' to 5' of twine, nylon string, or wire

A covering for the pit made of rubber, leather skins, a sheet of metal, a flat stone, or a thin sheet of plywood (the latter two make better drums than bows)

Shovel

Stones, stakes, or tent pegs

PROCEDURE

1. Dig a semi-round or conical-shaped pit in the earth one to two feet deep.

2. Implant the pole securely in the ground so that when it is flexed, the end reaches over the pit (A).

3. Punch a hole in the center of the chosen membrane and tie string through this hole (B) attached to a small stick or nail.

4. Secure membrane which covers the pit to the ground with stakes or heavy stones around the edge of the hole.

5. Flex pole and tie loose end of string near end of pole (C).

TO PLAY

Hold the flexible end of the stick in one hand and pluck or strum the string with the other hand.

Different pitches are produced by increasing and decreasing the tension of the string.

A second player can play directly on the skin-covering with drum sticks.

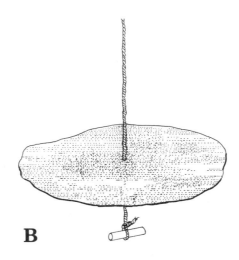

B

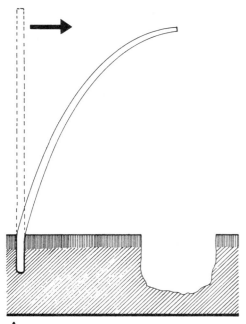

A

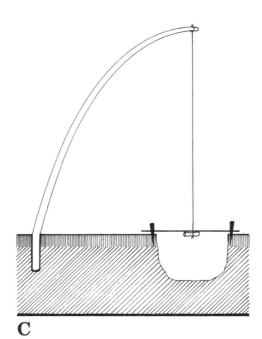

C

Washtub Bass

The washtub bass or "gut bucket" is a delightful instrument found usually in jug bands and other "down home" musical groups. It is a close cousin to the ground bow and probably more practical as an accompanying instrument. An amazingly solid bass line can be coaxed from this instrument with just a little practise.

MATERIALS
Metal washtub, metal wastebasket, two-gallon oil or turpentine can, or any large tin can at least 15" in diameter. Cardboard can be used but plastic is not as good

Heavy string, 3' or 4' long (nylon cord or thin clothesline is fine, baling twine is excellent)

30" to 36" dowel, depending on your height, broomstick, hockey stick, or other stick, 3/4" in diameter

Wooden peg or piece of dowel

TOOLS
Saw

Hammer

Drill with 1/4" bit

ASSEMBLY
1. Drill a hole through one end of the stick about 1" from the end (A).

2. Saw a groove in the other end perpendicular to the direction of the hole. This groove will notch on the rim of the bucket (B).

3. Punch a hole in the center of the bottom part of the bucket.

4. Tie a small wooden peg or dowel to one end of the string.

5. Thread the string through the hole in the bottom from inside to outside (C).

6. Tie the free end of the string through the hole in the stick.

TO PLAY
1. Hook the notched end of the stick over the rim of the bucket.

2. Brace the bucket by putting your right foot on the opposite rim.

3. Tighten or loosen the tension of the string by gently moving the stick backward and forward with your left hand. This will cause the pitch of the sound to change.

4. As you pluck the string with your right hand, slowly pull back on the stick to get the feel of its range.

5. Now, loosen the string until it ceases to make a clear sound.

6. Place a piece of wood under one edge of the tub to hold it just away from the floor. This will enable the bass to resonate better.

7. Pluck with a glove on your right hand to keep from wearing the skin off your fingers during heavy sessions.

PLAYING SUGGESTIONS
A nice characteristic of the washtub bass is that the pitch need not be exact to get the desired effect. Under practised hands, the tub bass can lay down a very accurate line — as can be witnessed by listening to recordings of good jug bands. The most important factor, though, is the low rhythmic effect.

Used in conjunction with other stringed and rhythm instruments, the low "thumm . . . thumm . . . thumm" of the bass can be most colorful and can add a pleasing dimension to many folk tunes.

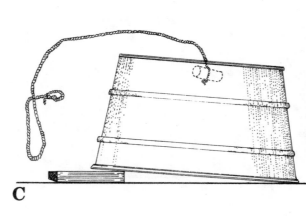

A-B   **C**

The bleach bottle banjo is part of a world-wide family of instruments that use the principle of a stick protruding through a resonator with any number of strings (even one string can yield beautiful music). The stick reaches from one end to the other of the resonator, while contacting the resonator through a bridge. These instruments can be plucked, strummed, or bowed.

MATERIALS

Plastic bleach bottle or other large plastic bottle — 2 to 4 qt. size. Large tin cans, large mailing tubes, paint buckets, or other containers also work well

30" length of wood 1" x 3"

About 3 yds. of nylon fishing line

Small piece of wood about 3/4" x 2" x 1/4" for the bridge

Two or three screw eyes (*optional*: dowel pegs or guitar tuners)

Two or three 1" finishing nails for hitch pins

TOOLS

Saw

Hammer

Utility knife

ASSEMBLY

1. Cut off the bottom half of the bottle (A). Cut an H-shaped slot the size of the wood strip starting about 1" from the bottom. The wood should fit tightly when the flaps of the bottle are folded out and the wood strip is inserted (B). The slots should be cut as close to the flat end of the bottle as possible.

2. Make an identical slot on the opposite side of the bottle.

3. Near one end of the stick, insert 2 or 3 screw eyes (C). Space the screw eyes so that the strings will be equidistant and will not interfere with each other.

4. Insert the stick through the bottle. Place a screw through the face of the bottle into the stick if necessary (D).

5. Place the same number of 1" finishing nails or small screw eyes on the other end of the stick (E).

6. Tie the string tightly between pairs of screw eyes.

7. Slide the small piece of wood under the strings and prop it up on edge (F). You may have to make a small notch for each string in the top of the bridge to keep the strings from sliding off.

8. To tune the strings, tighten or loosen them by turning the screw eyes. A nail inserted through the eye for leverage will aid in turning them.

You now have a fretless banjo. By stopping the string along the board neck with your fingers, you can pick out scales and melodies.

OPTIONS

Add a smaller bridge next to the tuning pegs (called a nut) to delineate a more precise string length (G). This can be accomplished by flattening a 1/4" dowel on one side and gluing it to the fingerboard. Notes of a major scale can either be marked on the fingerboard or as 1/4" dowels which are flattened on one side and glued to the fingerboard as frets (H). The nut should be notched and should raise the strings just enough to pass slightly above the first fret. If the

A

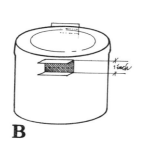

B

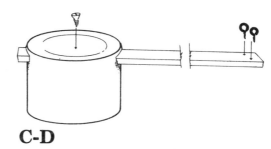

C-D

strings bump into frets farther down the fingerboard while fingering the first three or four frets, raise the height of the bridge slightly to correct this.

Paint or decorate the resonator to your liking.

PLAYING SUGGESTIONS

The bottle banjo is most effective in a rhythmic capacity; with some experimentation, however, musical variety may be coaxed from it. Practise is required to play a melody on a fretless instrument since the fingers have to be placed precisely. Each and every bottle banjo seems to have its own idiosyncrasies and must be explored individually.

A four-string instrument can draw on traditional banjo tunings for its orientation. Those with two or three strings might tune like a dulcimer (see p. 104). A major scale, for instance, would be tuned with the outside strings to the tonic pitch and the middle string to the dominant or the fifth scale degree. The melody is then fingered on the bottom string while strumming across the combined strings.

Finger picking styles are also effective. Listen to recordings of fretless banjos and you will be surprised at the variety and precision achieved.

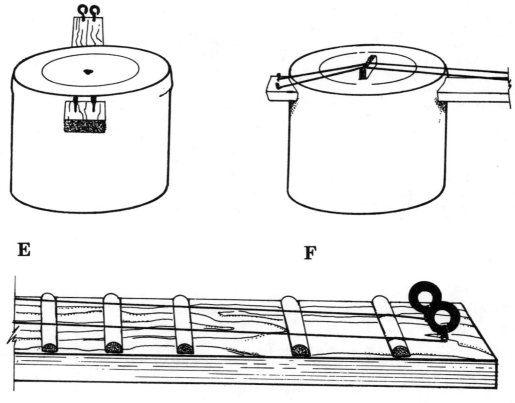

E

F

G-H

The board zither, or psaltery, is one of the most ancient instruments in civilized history. Examples all over the world have been fashioned in a variety of shapes and sizes. More popular members of this family include the autoharp of the United States and the Japanese koto. Even the harpsichord and modern piano show highly developed forms of this ancient family. Though most zithers are plucked, many (such as the piano) are tapped with mallets or hammers (as illustrated by the hammered dulcimer and its cousins around the world). The electric steel guitar, a fairly recent instrument, is a zither, sometimes with several fingerboards and pedals. The instrument described below is a very basic and easy-to-make form of the zither.

MATERIALS
One board 8" to 10" in length and about 3/4" thick by 6" to 8" wide (pine or plywood are sufficient or use a breadboard)

Nylon fishing line or metal guitar strings

8 nails with heads (about 1" long)

8 screw eyes

TOOLS
Hammer

Ruler

Saw

ASSEMBLY
1. Draw a line with a ruler about one inch from the end of the board. The line should be parallel to the end of the board (A).

2. Draw another line slanting from slightly over halfway up the side towards the opposite corner (B).

3. Hammer an evenly spaced row of nails partway into the board along the line drawn parallel to the end of the board.

4. Using a large nail to start the hole, insert a screw eye partway into the board along the other line opposite the nails (C). Any number of strings is acceptable. Try starting with just four or five and expand later to a full octave.

5. Attach the fishing line or guitar string firmly to the nail.

6. Pull the string tight and tie it or wrap it around the screw eye. Make the strings tighter by turning the screw eyes. Use a nail inserted through the screw eye as leverage for tuning.

7. Tune the strings to a scale with the help of a piano or pitch pipe. The strings will sound best if they are reasonably taut.

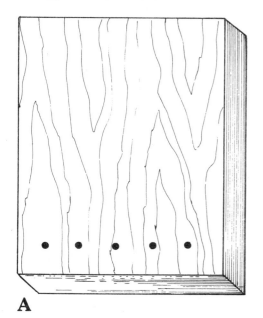

A

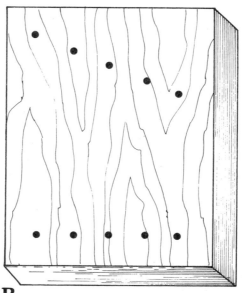

B

OPTIONS

The board zither has possibilities for decoration. You can paint or do wood-burn designs on the face of the board or drill holes in patterns like "sound-holes" under the strings.

PLAYING SUGGESTIONS

The strings may be tuned to a diatonic scale. A diatonic scale is equivalent to a "do-re-me-fa-sol-la-ti-do" arrangement. Or you can create your own exotic scale. Make sure that you are aware of how tight the strings are getting as you tune up. Otherwise there is a risk of breaking them. You may have to adjust to a lower scale if they become too tight or to a higher scale if they seem too loose.

Hold the zither in your left hand and put it next to your ear so that you can pluck the strings with your right hand. Melodies which are somewhat slow can be picked out as long as the range does not go beyond the one-octave span of the instrument. Fingers can do the plucking, although for a slightly sharper sound a guitar pick can be used.

The tuning may easily be changed to accommodate minor scales as well or it can be left in the original tuning and played modally.

Placing the board zither on a table or box helps to amplify the sound. Sound can also be amplified through a microphone.

A sound-box may be built onto the board for more resonance, but if you do this it is recommended that you use a thinner piece of wood for the top. Also, drilling a sound-hole in the top will increase the volume if a sound-box is incorporated. The instrument is meant to be a personal soft-sounding instrument.

Designs for a more sophisticated psaltery may be found later in this section (see page 27).

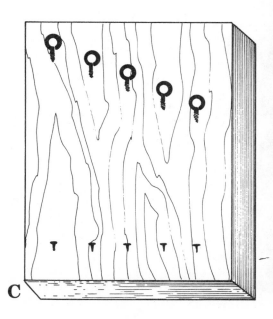

The stick "dulcimore" (or "dulciless," a term coined by Howie Mitchell) has its historical roots in the Appalachian Mountains of North America and is accounted as one of the very few truly American folk instruments. The instrument described below is a simplified version of the dulcimer, since it is lacking a soundbox.

One string (called the melody string) will do quite well for a beginner although the addition of another string or two can heighten the musical effect appreciably. If more than one string is used it is necessary for the staples to be placed under the first string only, the other one or two strings will act as drones.

MATERIALS

A 1" x 2" to 3/4" x 1-1/2" board about 30" long. Hardwoods are best but may offer some resistance to the staples. Pine and other softwoods are also suitable.

Two medium-sized screw eyes or pegs

1/4" dowel, sanded flat on one side, for bridge and nut

2-1st or 2nd guitar strings

2-1" nails

TOOLS

Hammer

Staple gun and staples

Glue

ASSEMBLY

1. Sand the wood smooth.

2. Draw lines on the board for the nut, bridge, and frets/staples according to diagram (A).

3. It will be quite difficult to insert the staples with complete accuracy, but put them in as carefully as possible. If the staples don't go all the way in, just give them a tap with a hammer. If they go in too far pry them up slightly with a screwdriver. They should stand up about a sixteenth of an inch above the surface of the board.

4. Flatten one side of each dowel and glue them to the board as shown in diagram (B). They should have exactly twenty-seven inches between their centers.

5. Put the screw eyes or pegs at one end as shown and the nails at the other, so that one string will pass over the frets (C).

6. Loop the string onto the nail and tie or wrap it around the screw eye securely.

7. Tune by turning the screw until the string sounds pleasant and is comfortably tight. You may have to use a dowel or nail for leverage (D).

8. Make a small notch in the nut and bridge to keep the string from slipping.

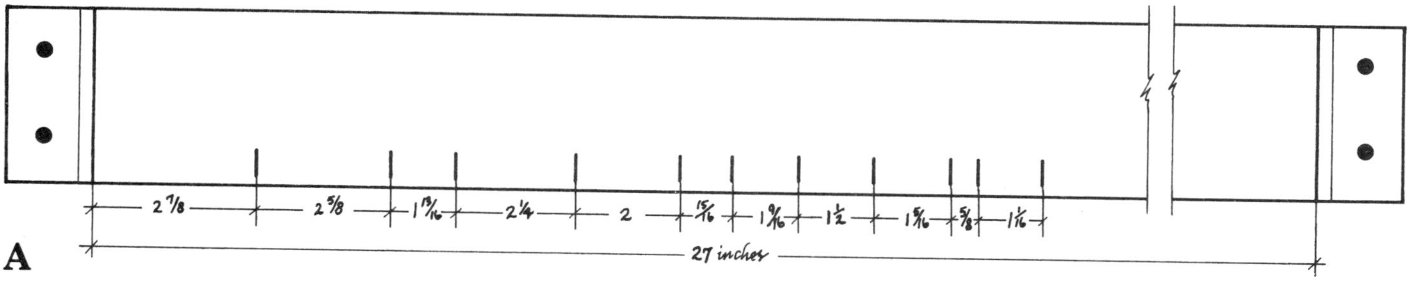
2 7/8
2 5/8
1 13/16
2 1/4
2
15/16
1 9/16
1 1/2
1 5/16
5/8
1 1/16
27 inches

A

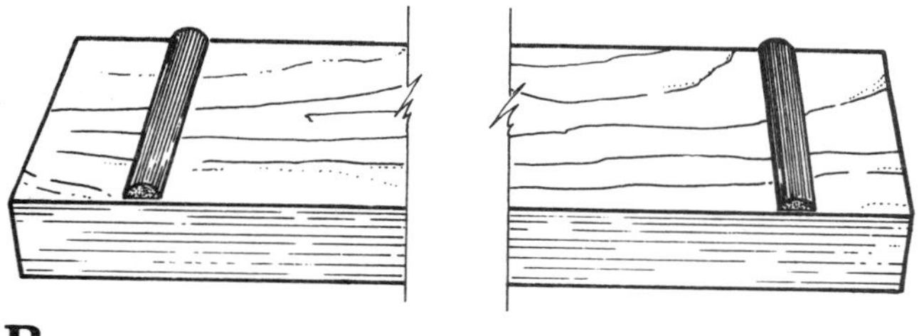

B

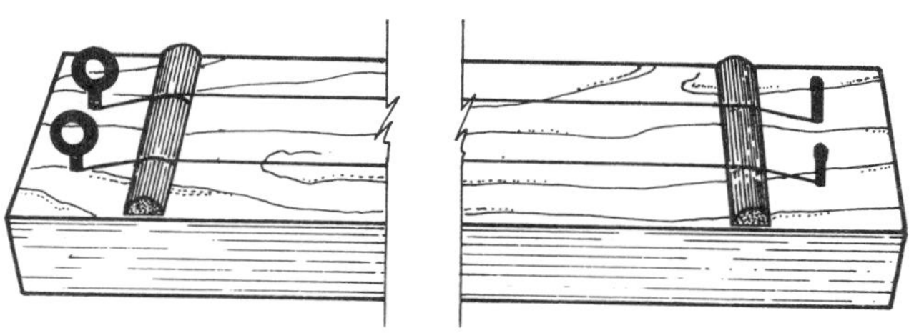

C

The string at the nut should be about 1/8" above the fingerboard and about 3/8" at the bridge.

D

PLAYING SUGGESTIONS
Two-Stringed Dulcimer

The staple/frets are laid out in a diatonic pattern. A diatonic scale is equivalent to a white key scale on the piano. It is simply a "do-re-me-fa-sol-la-ti-do" arrangement.

Noting is usually done with a 4" to 5" long by 1/4" thick dowel held firmly in the left hand. This "noter" slides from note to note, forming the melody. The right hand strums the appropriate rhythm with a guitar pick or a plectrum made from a plastic bottle. Traditionally, a goose or turkey quill shaved to a flat end has been used for strumming. The pick should be big enough to hold comfortably.

Tune the two strings in unison, to the same pitch. The dulcimer is a modal instrument and can achieve minor tonality by selecting, for instance, the fourth space as tonic (the "home base") and building a scale from that note. If your dulcimer has more than two strings, it is best to buy a dulcimer book which has all the tuning explanations.

As with the zither, if you place the stick on a desk top, or better yet on a cardboard box as you did with the zither, you will increase the volume appreciably. Some students have suggested placing an electronic pickup under the string. Other unusual effects could be created if a "fuzz" unit or even a "reverb" machine were attached.

Instructions on making more complicated dulcimers with sound-boxes are explained later in this book, see pp. 71 and 93.

The psaltery is a member of the zither family of stringed instruments. Globally, it spans an infinite number of shapes and sizes and playing techniques. The style of psaltery suggested here is an extension of an earlier instrument in this book — the board zither. The Western type of psaltery can be seen in many illustrated manuscripts of the Medieval and Renaissance periods during which time it enjoyed widespread popularity — that is, until the keyboard psaltries, such as the clavichord and harpsichord took precedence.

MATERIALS

A 13" x 12" section of 1/8" plywood

A 14" x 1" x 1" stick of maple or other hardwood for end blocks

A 20" x 1" x 1/2" stick of maple for the sides

A 14" x 1/2" x 3/8" strip of maple or other hardwood

12 zither pins and 12 hitch pins or 3/4" finishing nails

A 14" length of 3/32" steel rod or coat hanger (optional)

.014 and .016 music wire (guitar or banjo strings)

TOOLS

White glue

Saws (wood saw, coping, or fret saw, optional hacksaw)

Drill and bits to match zither pins and hitch pins

Clamps, weights, and/or rubber bands

Plane

Sandpaper and finishing materials

Tuning wrench

ASSEMBLY

1. Cut plywood into two equal pieces for top and bottom of psaltery (A). Some plywoods have only one "good" side. Cutting it in this manner ensures that the good sides are facing the outside of the box.

2. On the top piece draw a circle about 1-1/4" in diameter in the center (B). Either drill it out with a circle cutter or drill a small hole through which a coping saw blade or fret saw blade may be inserted. Reattach the blade to the saw and cut around penciled area. Sand smooth.

3. From the 14" x 1" x 1" stick cut two pieces for the end blocks. Cut the angles so they match the angles of the bottom piece of plywood (C).

4. Glue and weight end blocks. Let dry.

5. Cut the side pieces from the 20" x 1" x 1/2" hardwood stick so they fit down the sides of the instrument between the end blocks. Measure as you go so a good fit will result. Glue into place.

6. Glue on top and clamp, weight or rubber band to the sound-box (D). You may have to plane or sand the sides and end blocks to insure a good join with the top. Check this carefully before applying glue.

7. Cut the 14" x 1/2" x 3/8" strip into two pieces which will act as the bridges across the top one inch from each end

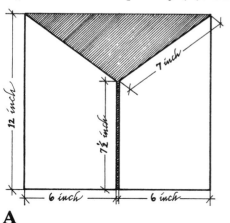

A

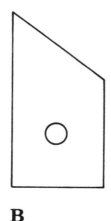

B

C

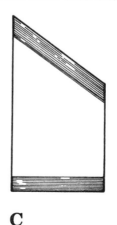

D

(E). Though not entirely necessary, a length of steel rod or coathanger is usually placed in a groove on top of the bridges to keep the strings from cutting into the wood (F). The groove may be cut by hand or cut with a small hobbiest router called a Dremel tool. Molding with a groove already cut may be found at a hardware store.

8. Glue the bridges in place. Weight and let dry.

9. Drill holes to receive the zither pins (G). Do a test on a scrap piece of wood first to make sure the hole will hold the pins firmly. The holes may be drilled at a slight angle (H).

10. Drill the holes to receive the hitch pins (I). Piano bridge pins are good for this purpose or 3/4" finishing nails may be used with good results. A better method, however, is to predrill the holes to prevent the wood from splitting.

11. Finish box by staining to the desired shade or by decorating with paint. Varnish or lacquer according to the instructions given on the container.

12. Screw in zither pins leaving enough protruding for a few more twists as strings are attached. You will need a matching tuning wrench for this purpose.

13. Gently hammer in hitch pins.

14. String by twos as shown (J). This method bypasses the necessity of tying a loop in the end of each string.

15. Place steel rod in the bridge grooves.

16. Tune. You will find that several tunings may be necessary before the strings settle in and stabilize. It may be easiest to tune to a piano or have a musician help you with the initial tuning.

PLAYING SUGGESTION

Play melodically in the same fashion suggested for the board zither, see p. 23. As chords, two- and three-note harmonies are quite effective. Try plucking strings 1, 3, and 5 either simultaneously or as a broken configuration followed by moving two fingers up so that strings 1, 4, and 6 sound. Back to 1, 3, 5 then pluck strings 2, 4, and 5 and finally to 1, 3, and 5 again. This is called a I-IV-I-V-I (1-4-1-5-1) progression and is the basis for many songs.

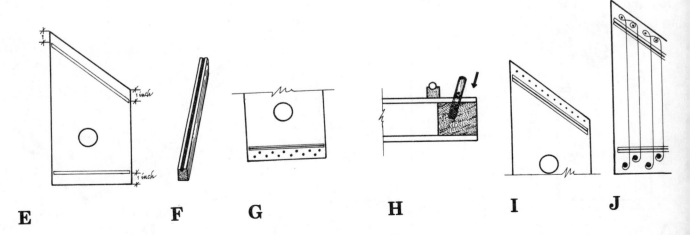

E   F   G   H   I   J

Historically, the range of wind instruments is as rich as that of stringed instruments. Their use dates back well into prehistoric times as evidenced by the remains of bone flutes and conch shell horns that have been unearthed. Through the centuries, wind instruments have been used to signify special happenings or reserved for occasions of unusual significance. The triumphant marching of the Roman conquerors was always accompanied by music from long exotically curved trumpets. One might also consider the compelling flute music of the Pied Piper which cast spells of enchantment over animals and humans or the shattering and powerful horns of Gabriel in the Biblical heralding of the final judgment day. In contemporary times brass and winds have also been used to lead armies to war, to inspire nationalistic fervor, and to add pomp and splendor to festive occasions. As well, wind instruments have found use in more intimate circumstances. American Indians made individually scaled flutes and composed delicate songs to court their chosen women. East Indians also used the flute and their subtly embellished music has given that instrument a mystic quality that is undeniable.

Wind instruments are acoustically more difficult to understand than stringed instruments because while you can see a string vibrate, you cannot readily see what happens when you vibrate a column of air. There is also a special technique for "blowing" wind instruments and this varies with different instruments.

There are commonly three categories of wind instruments: flutes, reeds, and horns. Flutes and whistles include those instruments with a small "blow hole" towards one end and a series of finger holes arranged in a variety of patterns down the length of the instrument. In flutes such as the Irish penny whistle and recorder the air is blown through a mouthpiece which forces the air to split over a sharp edge thus producing the sound. Some flutes such as the three-holed penny whistle are meant to be played with one hand while the other hand plays the rhythm on a small drum. In contrast to this the flute found in a modern orchestra shows a high technical evolution with its many keys, levers, and mechanisms. Flutes are found in all parts of the world and are made from such diverse materials as wood, bamboo, stone, and human and animal bones.

Reed instruments, as their name denotes, utilize thin flexible reeds activated by air for tone production. Children use the reed principle when they squeeze the end of a soda straw and place it between their lips to make it produce a squawk. The highly sophisticated oboe and English horn work on the same principle. An unusual variation includes the Scottish bagpipes where air is blown into a leather bag and then squeezed through a series of pipes which have reeds inside. This arrangement gives a constant uninterrupted sound.

Horn and trumpet players vibrate or "buzz" their lips into a cup-shaped mouthpiece to produce sound. The original horns of which the ram's horn and the conch shell are members depended on the tightening and loosening of the lips for different pitch. Later, holes were added to achieve greater variety. Eventually modern construction techniques added valves, slides, and tubing to facilitate the movement of sounds. The descriptions that follow begin with projects of a simple and experimental nature and progress to examples that are more challenging.

Pen Cap Pipes

Collect all the ballpoint and felt-tip pen caps you can find. Blow strongly across the open end of each cap until you can produce a pitch. Change the angle of blowing slightly if you have difficulty making them speak. (Some pen caps may be too small to give a clear pitch.) Arrange them high to low and tape them together so you have a set of pen cap Pan pipes to give various pitches (A). Create a simple tune.

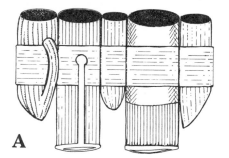

A

Straw Oboe

Find some waxed paper straws or plastic straws. Paper ones work best. Flatten about one inch of one end of the paper straw and snip off a little of the corners with scissors (A). If you use plastic straws, flatten about 2" and slit about 1" down the crease with a knife. Snip the corners.

Put the cut end into your mouth just past your lips and blow. Keep trying and adjusting a little farther into or out of your mouth until you get a good squawk. Try poking a finger hole or two into the straw and see if you can produce a simple scale (B). Cut other straws to different lengths and have your friends squawk along in harmony.

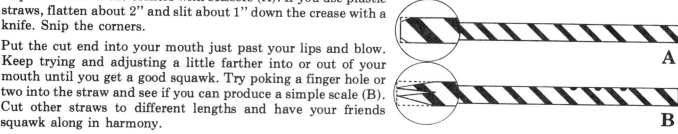

A

B

Comb and Tissue Kazoo

Fold a piece of tissue paper or wax paper over a comb (A). Place the flat side of the comb to your lips and hum through the paper. The buzzing quality will add a new dimension to your songs.

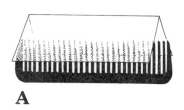

A

Blade Whistle

Place a blade of grass or a thin strip of paper between the edges of your thumbs so that the blade is held snugly between the two knuckles and a blow hole is created between them (A). Hold it to your mouth so you can blow through the passage onto the edge of the grass or paper blade. Blow fairly hard. It may need adjustment or renewal after a few blows. A good squawk or screech should result.

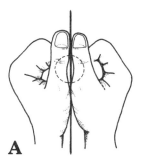

A

Jugs

The jug band style of music got its name from the tuba-like sound of the whiskey jug pumping out a type of rhythmic bass line. A bleach bottle (well cleaned) or a ceramic jug produces a deep pitch when air is blown across the spout opening. Buzzing the lips loosely as you blow creates a new quality of sound. Pitches may be produced by tightening and loosening the lips slightly. Blow in a rhythmic fashion.

Bottles

Blow across the tops of milk bottles, pop bottles, wine or beer bottles for a variety of sounds and pitches. Bottles with smaller openings are easiest to blow. By adding certain volumes of water to a row of bottles you can actually create a scale which will allow you to play melodies. Adding water makes the volume of air in the bottle smaller and thus raises the pitch produced. Have your friends blow different rhythms on different sized bottles for variety in sounds.

Bull Roarer

Tie a 3' length of good strong string or twine through a hole drilled in one end of a ruler-like piece of wood about 3/8" x 2" x 10" (A). The wood should be basically flat but not too wide or long. This is a bull roarer.

Swing the bull roarer overhead until it begins to spin in the air causing a roaring sound. The speed of swing and the size of the wood control the pitch.

Note Be sure to have plenty of swinging room and to make all knots secure.

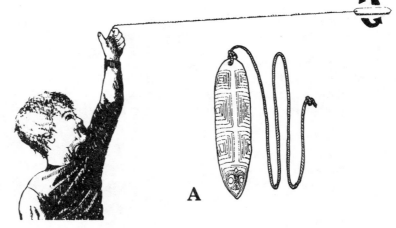

A

The hose bugle has been used occasionally by a classical brass player as a musical joke; however, the instrument is capable of producing true pitches and actual music. Dennis Brain, a late great French horn player, could play Mozart on the hose bugle with a great degree of accuracy.

MATERIALS
A length of hose (3' to 10' of garden hose will do)

A trumpet or other brass instrument mouthpiece (optional)

A funnel (plastic or metal)

Masking tape

PROCEDURE
1. Secure the funnel on one end of the hose by wrapping masking tape around the narrow part of the funnel and jamming it into the end of the hose or place the funnel into the hose and wrap masking tape around the point where they connect.

Note The metal connectors may be left on or removed.

2. On the other end simply use the metal connector as the mouthpiece or find a trumpet (or other brass instrument) mouthpiece and secure it as you did the funnel.

TO PLAY
Buzz your lips into the mouthpiece and try changing the pitch by tightening and loosening your lip pressure slightly. Play the instrument like a bugle. If you find this difficult try to find a brass player and have him give you a demonstration.

Horns such as these have been used throughout history as signaling horns because of their audible range. In ancient times they were probably used to start charges into battle or signal the arrival of a stranger. They were also used while hunting so that members of a hunting party would know where and when game was found.

Hunting Horn

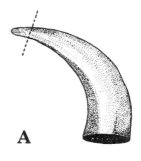

A

MATERIALS
One cow's horn or other animal horn

Trumpet mouthpiece (bugle or cornet mouthpieces are excellent)

TOOLS
Saw

Knife

Drill and bit (the bit size is determined by the shank size of the mouthpiece)

PROCEDURE
1. Find a horn from a crafts store, taxidermist, veterinarian or, if all else fails, a slaughterhouse. If you obtain a fresh animal horn you must process it as follows:

a) Set up a small fire or camp stove *outside* and boil the horn for a couple of hours or until marrow is soft.

b) Scrape and carve out all the marrow from the inside.

c) Sand and polish horn inside and out until smooth and shiny.

2. Cut off pointed end of horn a little at a time (A) until the mouthpiece shank fits snugly into the hole or, cut off end and drill a hole into the end so the mouthpiece will fit (B).

OPTIONS
If the horn is large and thick, a cup-shaped recess may be carved directly into the end of the horn thus bypassing the need of a trumpet mouthpiece (C). However, the carved recess should resemble the shape of a trumpet mouthpiece.

TO PLAY
Use the same procedure suggested for the hose bugle.

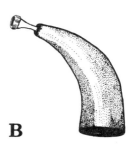

B

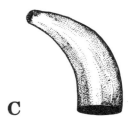

C

34 Willow Whistle

The willow whistle has been a part of woods lore for a long time and it makes a great old-fashioned toy. There are a number of variations that may be used to make this instrument. If you ever have the opportunity, ask a wood whittler how he makes his whistle.

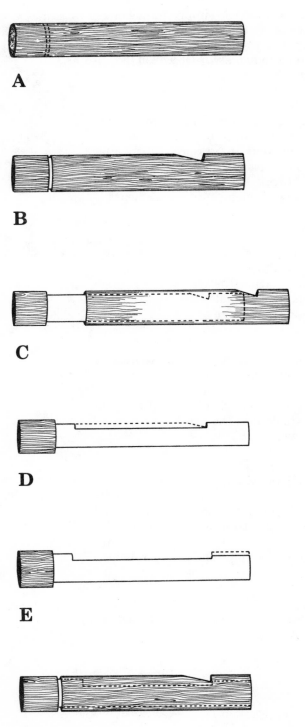

MATERIALS

A piece of willow about 5" to 8" long and about 1" in diameter or any *smooth-barked* wood except maple, hickory, or oak. Ash works well if willow is not available. It is best to make this whistle in the spring when the sap is running and the bark will slip off easily.

PROCEDURE

1. Measure about an inch or two from the end and cut around through the bark *only* (A). The portion with the bark left on is the handle and will make peeling easier when it comes time to pull the bark off.

2. Cut off the other end evenly. From this end measure about 3/4" and cut a notch approximately 1/2" deep (B).

3. Tap and rub bark with the handle of your knife until the bark loosens and eventually slides off (C). Twisting the bark off sometimes helps but be sure not to crack and break the bark while maneuvering. Wetting will often help loosen the bark.

4. Cut a long channel from the blow hole to within 1/2" or so from the end where the bark was left on (D).

5. Slice off a little strip from the top of the blowing end to allow an air passage (E).

6. Replace bark onto core and line up the blow hole with the long notch. Blow gently (F).

7. Adjust by trimming more wood from the air passage into the channel.

TO PLAY

Achieve a variety of pitches by cupping your hands over the blow hole which will slightly choke and lower the pitch. Open hands slowly and pitch will rise a little.

Pan pipes are a set of end blown flutes arranged in various numbers and combinations. They have been made in sets of two pipes to as many as sets of twenty-five or more. Sometimes called Pan's pipes after the Greek god of forests, pastures, and shepherds, Pan pipes are presently most popular in the folk music of Hungary, Peru, and Africa.

MATERIALS

About 5' of stiff plastic tubing with a diameter of 3/8" to 1"

Bamboo is used in most authentic pipes of this sort

Plugs for the tubes (rubber stoppers, cork, or plasticine clay will work)

Tape or glue to hold pipes together

TOOLS

Sharp knife or saw if bamboo is used (see options)

Ruler

ASSEMBLY

1. Keep in mind the simple principle that the longer the pipe, the lower the pitch. You can make a set of pipes of any number of individual pipes of whatever lengths you like. Interesting scale combinations can be created in this fashion. Adjustments of the pitch can be made by trimming off a little length at a time or by pushing the stoppers farther into the tube. Note, however, that you cannot make the pipes lower by adding on if too much is cut off. If this happens, save the pipe for the next higher pitch and cut a new segment.

2. If you prefer, cut a set that makes a specific scale. Pan pipes are most often found in this form. You may do this by ear or use the following measurements as a guide. These lengths should approximate a G major scale if a 5/8" diameter tubing is used.

do	8-3/8"	sol	5-3/8"
re	7-1/2"	la	4-3/4"
me	6-1/2"	ti	4-1/4"
fa	6"	do	4"

OPTIONS

If you make the pipes of bamboo you may have to drill through the natural joints of the wood to get the proper lengths or you can use the joints as the stopped end and trim from the other end to the desired pitch (A). The pipes may be glued together for more stability. A decorative strip of cloth can be glued around the pipes. Sticks may be laced on either side of the tubes (B) to give a varied decorative effect.

PLAYING SUGGESTIONS

To hear the Pan pipes played well is a most amazing experience. South Americans, for instance, play them with great facility and speed. Playing the Pan pipes involves the same blowing technique as blowing into a bottle. With a little practise in moving the pipes accurately across the mouth opening, some facility can be developed. It takes a lot of wind to play the pipes so take a deep breath as often as necessary.

Note You can hand out single pipes to a group of people and play them in the fashion of hand bells. Each person can be responsible for a pitch or two within the song thus co-ordinating the efforts into a coherent melody.

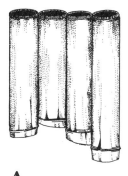

A

B

Pipe Recorder

This member of the flute family has a soft gentle tone reminiscent of the simple shepherd's pipe. During the Medieval and Renaissance periods, different sizes of pipes were combined into families or consorts and many pieces were composed for this melodious choir.

Making recorders and flutes requires patience and a bit of luck, so be prepared to experiment and refine as you proceed.

MATERIALS
Stiff plastic tube, garden hose, or bamboo about 12" long with an inside diameter of approximately 3/4"

Cork or wooden dowel the same diameter as the inside of the tube

TOOLS
Sharp knife (a saw or file should be used for bamboo)

3/16" to 1/4" drill bit and drill

Sandpaper

Small round file

Small saw

ASSEMBLY
1. If using bamboo, clear out joints carefully with a brace and bit.

2. Measure 1" from the end and cut the "flue" hole as diagrammed (A). It may be easier to use the file or saw on bamboo.

3. Take a piece of dowel or cork that fits snugly into the hose and sand or cut one side as shown (B). It is easiest to place the sandpaper flat on the table and work the dowel to shape (C).

4. Place the plug into the end of the pipe so that the slanted surface inclines towards the flue hole as shown (D).

5. Insert the plug so that it ends right at the flue opening so that the air will rush through the narrow channel and split over the sharp end of the flue hole (D).

If you are very lucky, a soft blow will produce a clear note. If it doesn't play well at first, move the plug backward or forward in the tube. If it blows hard, try sanding off the slant a little bit at a time. If it blows easy enough but with no response, try sanding the slant a little steeper. There is a danger of sanding off too much, in which case you need to get another piece of dowel or cork and start over. However, there is no need to do that unless you've tried everything else.

HOLE PLACEMENT
1. Experimenting with hole placement can be a very creative experience. Many cultures in the world have created their own tonal systems which sound quite exotic to Western ears. For example, individuals in certain Indian tribes are especially revered for their flute playing. Personal scales are created by these individuals and these become their musical trademark.

2. If you desire a tuned scale, before you add any holes, tune the pipe to around C by cutting off a little at a time from the end opposite the mouthpiece.
Note   There are many variables to consider when making a *tuned* pipe. Be prepared to experiment.

3. Draw a straight line the length of the pipe from the center of the flue hole to the open end (E).

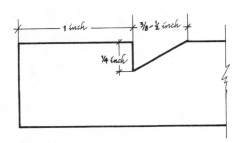

A

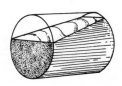

B

C

4. With the 1/4" bit, drill your first hole approximately 1-1/2" to 2" from the open end (opposite the mouthpiece).

5. Tune the note to a D. If it is sharp, file a little off the bottom part of the hole or if it is flat, file a little from the top part. If by accident the hole becomes too enlarged or flat, add a bit of tape over part of the hole to correct it.

6. Drill and tune each hole one at a time using the measurements below (F).

7. Notice the thumb hole opposite the other hole so that a full octave may be achieved.

PLAYING SUGGESTIONS

If you are making your own scale patterns each pattern may consist of any number of notes you wish. As you add notes experiment with your recorder:
1. Try blowing very soft while moving your fingers.
2. Blow very hard and see what effects you can produce.
3. Slide fingers slowly off notes.
4. Try different combinations of fingers.
5. Compose a tune in your own special tonal system.

If you have made a recorder tuned to a major scale, begin by covering all the holes (making sure the holes are *completely* covered) and blow softly. Lift one finger at a time until all the holes are open, then, by covering all the holes again and blowing harder you may be able to play a higher-pitched scale using the same procedure.

Try playing a simple song or nursery tune after your initial explorations. If any particular note is out of tune, you may temper the note by filing as suggested earlier or by adding tape to the edge of the faulty finger hole.

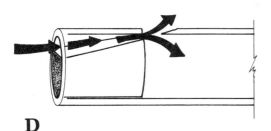

D

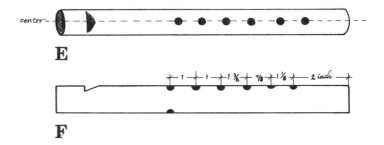

E

F

Slide Whistle

The slide whistle is a distant relative of the slide trombone. The pitch is changed by actually varying the length of the tube with a plunger instead of with finger holes.

MATERIALS

One foot of firm plastic tubing

A piece of doweling that will fit the inside diameter of the tube for the mouthpiece. A store-bought mouthpiece may be taped or glued onto the tubing if you wish.

A length of 3/8" doweling a bit longer than the tube to be used for the slider

A small scrap of plastic sponge about 1/2" thick

Glue

ASSEMBLY

1. Cut a circle out of the sponge just slightly larger than the tube.

2. Glue the sponge to the end of the dowel slide (A). Let the glue dry.

3. Fit the sponge slide tightly inside the tube so that it slides smoothly. Adjust if necessary. A strip of felt or leather may be glued around the dowel as a seal instead of using the sponge.

4. Carefully cut the air hole, shape the dowel, and test the mouthpiece as described for the pipe recorder (see pp. 36, 37) or tape on a factory-made whistle mouthpiece.

5. Stabilize the slide by adding a cork or hardwood plug at the end opposite the mouthpiece with a hole drilled in it slightly larger than the slider (B). This will keep the slide from being too loose. If you use a slider that is only slightly smaller than the inside diameter of the tube, this step may not be necessary (C).

PLAYING SUGGESTIONS

The slide whistle has always been a favorite with children because of its obvious special sliding qualities. It can sometimes also be utilized musically for that characteristic. In the right hands it can also be a relatively controlled instrument capable of a wide range of expression. Melodies may be played by listening carefully and moving the slide with reasonable accuracy from note to note. It is an effect that could be used to add tonal color to the appropriate song to achieve a wailing or haunting mood. Primarily, though, it is meant to be a fun instrument for "tootling" around.

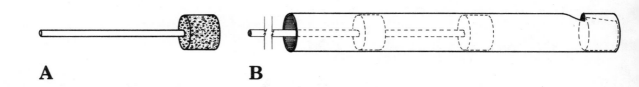

A   B

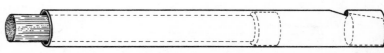

C

Flutes are probably one of the oldest and most ubiquitous of wind instruments. They come in a tremendous range of sizes and materials. Stone, metal, wood, ceramic, bone, bamboo, and reed flutes have been seen throughout history in almost every culture in the world. Some flutes are even played through the nose.

MATERIALS
Plastic pipe (plumber's PCV pipe, any plastic pipe with a fairly thin-walled construction, bamboo or wooden tube, and thin-walled metal tubing will work well). The pipe or tube should be about 1' to 1-1/2" long, 3/4" diameter.

A cork that will fit into the end of the pipe

TOOLS
Saw or tube-cutter to cut tube to length

Drill with a 1/4" or a 5/16" bit

A vise or someone to help hold the tube while drilling

Round file

ASSEMBLY
1. Place the cork in the end of the pipe (A). It must be a tight seal.

2. Cut the pipe to length.

3. Drill the blow hole about 2" from the end. Experiment with size and shape (patiently) until you or a flautist can get a sound. The hole should be in an oval shape about 3/8" across (B). Give it a slightly chamfered edge if it does not respond (C).

4. Experiment with how far the cork fits into the end of the tube. Some flutes place it right up close to the blow hole whereas others leave it well recessed from the blow hole.

MAKING A SCALE
You can create your own personal scale by placing finger holes along the flute to conform to your hands and fingertips.

1. Start with a hole at the end opposite the mouthpiece and test it.

2. Drill another hole about 1" higher and experiment with that.

3. Add as many holes as seem feasible with about 1" between each hole. The thumb can have a hole too.

Making a Major Scale
As with the pipe recorder, making a major scale requires very precise mea-surements. Fourteen inches of a 3/4" PCV pipe with holes at the following prescribed points should result in a B-flat major scale (D).

1. Drill each hole carefully and directly in the center of each dot.

2. You might consider placing a dowel inside the tube to keep the drill from slipping through to the other side.

OPTION
Paint your flute or wrap decorative threading around it with a spot of glue at the beginning and end of each thread to hold it in place.

PLAYING SUGGESTIONS
One of the major problems with playing the flute is that it takes a great deal of patience to get a consistent tone and to achieve some degree of breath control. Sometimes it takes weeks before a child can finally make a sound. But the music is rewarding and the extra effort is worthwhile.

Blow very gently across the blow hole, not into it. Place the flute to your mouth so the lower lip barely touches the blow hole, then roll it ever so slightly away and blow gently to the opposite side of the blow hole. Don't worry about the fingers until you can make a sound and hold it for a length of time.

The flute is usually held as shown.

If your flute is not exactly in tune, don't worry about it, for it will still have its own unique color and character. If you want to correct any bad notes, follow the procedure described for the pipe recorder (see pp. 36, 37).

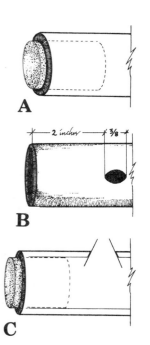

A

B

C

D

Instruments designed to be tapped and struck come in such variety of shapes and sizes that the imagination is the only limit to their conception. Instruments such as the drum utilize stretched membranes for their effect. Drums are variously shaped and are made from a wide array of materials. Many of the acoustical principles previously discussed apply to drums as well. As in stretched strings, for example, the pitch depends on the size and weight of the membrane and the amount of tension under which it is held. The loudness or amplitude of the sound depends on the force of the blow. The tone depends on the materials from which both the drum and the "beaters" are made.

Cymbals, gongs, and bells have a rather obscure physics and vibrate in a more complex fashion than one might think. Most bells are made of metal, but other materials such as glass have produced sounds of great beauty. Tubular bells or chimes are found in most churches.

Those instruments which depend on a stiff bar or rod also have their own characteristics and depend to a large extent on the acoustical principles discussed previously. Glockenspiels, chime bars, xylophones, and similar instruments are placed in this category.

There is also a large group of instruments that rely mostly on a unique tone quality or rhythmic timbre for their effect. Quite often these types do not produce a pure or recognizable pitch but their "voice" does add the spice and tonal variety to an otherwise drab composition. This list of noise makers is endless and includes such items as shakers and rattles (maracas), rasps (guiro), clackers (claves and castanets), jingles (tambourine), and many more.

Experimentation in this area will reveal much practical information.

Percussion instruments add great color and intensity to any musical ensemble whether it be a Brahms symphony or a primitive rite. There is virtually no end to the combinations of sounds that can be achieved with rhythm instruments. Each instrument is capable of a number of tonal effects de-

pending on how it is held, what it is struck with, and how it is struck. It is possible to develop the dynamic range of these instruments to give music that extra dimension — the rise and fall that makes music effective.

Perhaps you have been involved in a spontaneous happening when someone begins tapping a rhythm on some object and another person adds a little syncopation. When sounds enter, patterns begin to evolve, the sounds rise to a climax and then relax for a new breath. New variations are often added, such as finding something in the room that produces pitches while someone else begins a rudimentary melody over the established beat and another will begin to "hoot" on a bottle or tap partially filled glasses for more and more variety. These can be fun experiences. If you are particularly fortunate you may have had the opportunity to attend an Indian pow wow where four or five men in a circle around one large drum pound an incessant beat under a chant while men, women, and children move in step around the circle. Such persuasive beating can have a hypnotic and powerful effect.

Listen closely to an Indian raga and you will hear that the two little drums called "tabla" are capable of incredible intensity. Starting slowly then building, they achieve an unbelievable number of sounds. Or find a recording of an African ceremony where log drums are used to weave complex patterns of rhythm while tribe members dance to the compelling beat.

We've all been caught up in this rhythmical intensity at one time or another. Rhythm is probably one of the most powerful components of music. Anyone can relate to it. Anyone can make a simple beat. Rhythms can be simple, yet remain effective. The hands, the feet, and the mouth can be great rhythm instruments and these have the advantage of being highly portable.

Washboard

The washboard has always been a popular percussion instrument in jug bands of the Appalachian Mountain region and can be adapted to a wide range of folk music. All you need to make this instrument is a washboard with metal ridges, one to three thimbles, a wire hair brush, or a stick. Optional attachments might include bicycle bells, horns, and rattles. Paint is optional.

Paint all the framing of the washboard. Do not paint the metal ribbing. Attach the noisemakers with screws or glue.

If you are using thimbles, cover fingers and tap and rub rhythmically along the metal ridges of the washboard. The wooden frame may be tapped for variety. The same basic procedure should be used for the wire hair brush and stick. In addition to rubbing and tapping the primary beat of the song, add off-beat rhythms and syncopations. The washboard is usually played for fast tempo or highly rhythmic songs. If you incorporate bells and horns, use them sparingly as surprises or humorous effects.

Some players make a harness so they can hang the board around their necks and play with both hands. For added ideas listen to jug band recordings for the washboard.

Bones

A

Bones have been used in many types of music for a rhythmic castanet effect. A pair of bones in each hand of the proficient player will add a fancy touch to a quick-paced tune. Use a pair of sparerib bones, soap, and a scouring pad. Make sure you clean the bones thoroughly and dry them. You could wax or decorate them if you desired.

Hold the bones loosely on either side of the middle finger. The palm should be facing down and the bones should dangle between the fingers about three-quarters of their length (A). Shake or rattle them against each other using the thumb and fourth finger to help control the rhythm.

Spoons

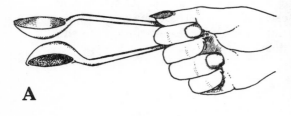

A

Spoons are an Appalachian-style instrument used to add rhythmic spice to any spirited song. Use two ordinary metal spoons. No preparation is needed. Different types of spoons give different effects. Many musicians prefer spoons with a broad curved-up end to help anchor them in the hand. Soup spoons are often recommended.

Place spoons on either side of the index finger with cupped sides facing away from each other and stems planted firmly into the palm (A). Rattle rapidly between your thigh and other hand in different rhythms. Try not to overuse or the effect may become fatiguing on the ears. Experiment with different sized spoons until you find the size that suits you best.

Rhythm sticks may be made from any material that can be tapped together to add a new element of sound and rhythm to appropriate songs. Experiment and use your imagination. You could use varying sizes and lengths of doweling, wooden spoons, segments of bamboo, broom handle sticks, plastic tubing, spare-rib bones, branches of a tree, metal rods or pipes, or railroad spikes.

If you use sticks, strike the sticks (of different sizes and materials) to determine which ones resonate best. Experiment with different lengths. Sand the edges or corners round. Decorate if you wish.

Hold one implement in your left hand and tap with the other stick. If you cup the left hand slightly and hold the stick (or whatever) *loosely* it will give a more resonant sound (A).

A

Scrapers and Rasps

There are many uses for these special effect music makers. To make them you will need two pieces of wood of any manageable size and different sizes of doweling. About 1/4" to 1" diameter works well but any shape of scrap about 10" long will do. Notch one length of wood with fairly deep grooves about 1/8" apart. The notches can be on one side or all around the stick and can be in patterns if you wish (A). If left smooth, the other stick may be of a smaller size than the notched piece. Sand both pieces, rounding edges and ends.

Play your instruments by rubbing the smaller stick along the notched stick. Try rubbing in different rhythms and at different speeds. To enhance the effect, place the end of the notched stick on a turned-over bucket or washtub and stroke with the smooth stick. The bucket will act as a sound-box and amplify the sound.

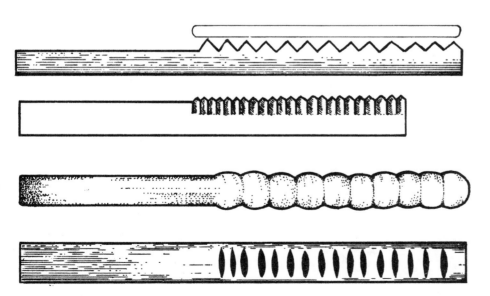

A

44 Sandpaper Blocks

This is another type of scraper that is used in children's rhythm bands.

MATERIALS

Two small blocks of pine or plywood, approximately 1" x 4" x 5" (although size is not really that important)

Sandpaper (experiment with different grades of sandpaper to make different effects.

Thumbtacks

Thread spools and glue or cabinet knobs and screws

ASSEMBLY

1. Cover one side of each block with sandpaper.

2. Fold the sandpaper over the edges and fasten it with thumbtacks. Cut the corners out so sandpaper will fold neatly around the block (A).

3. Trim off excess.

4. Glue or screw handles to the other side of each block (B).

PLAYING SUGGESTIONS

Rub the blocks together in a continuous motion for a swishing, whispering sound or bring the blocks together in a more percussive manner for a more rhythmic effect.

A   B

Rattles

Any container that can be sealed and easily handled makes a good rattle; anything that will move freely inside the container completes the instrument. The size, shape, and material of the container, along with what is inside, will influence the sound quality of the rattle.

CONTAINER SUGGESTIONS

Soft drink, beer, or juice cans or tennis ball can

Paper cups with lids

Plastic soap or bleach bottles

Small plastic or cardboard boxes, such as matchboxes

Glass food jars

Gourds

Coconut shell

Balloon

Metal boxes

CONTENT SUGGESTIONS

Rice or macaroni

Rocks, pebbles, or gravel

Marbles

Sand

Beans, seeds, or popcorn

BB's and birdshot

OPTION

Wedge or screw a dowel or stick into or onto the container for a handle. You will find the rattle more resonant if the actual container is not held in the hand.

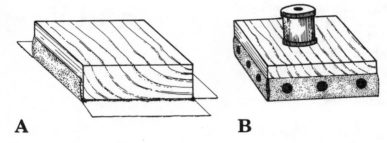

This elaborate jingle originated in Turkey for use in military exercises. It found its way through Europe and finally into the United States where it was used in poor regions as an effective rhythmic instrument.

MATERIALS
Broom handle

Lots of metal bottle caps

3/4" round-headed nails

OPTIONS
Bells, cymbals, bicycle horns, drums, and any other clangers and bangers that you can attach

ASSEMBLY
1. Remove all the cork or plastic out of the bottle caps.

2. Punch a hole through the center of each cap.

3. Nail the caps from the tip to bottom so that all are free to shake. (Don't forget to leave room to hold the stick.)

4. Put a rubber door stopper or crush tip on the bottom of the pole so that the hard "thump" will be softened when the pole is struck against the floor.

5. More bells and jingles can be accommodated if cross pieces are attached to the main pole. Or hang bells around the rim of a tin can and attach it to the pole by poking a hole through the bottom of the can and inserting it onto the pole.

PLAYING SUGGESTIONS
Thump the stick rhythmically against the floor and shake it in the air. If horns and drums are used, utilize them for special effects. The visual aspect of the jingling johnnie is quite important so the more design creations and fancy playing styles you can concoct the more spectacular the impression.

One of the fanciest rattles of this sort is known as the Turkish crescent. This instrument was used by Turkish armies to heighten the effect of their marching by creating a steady and unearthly clamor that must have been fearsome indeed! The concept of the Turkish crescent is similar to the jingling johnnie but with certain stylized components such as the crescent and moon which have special significance in Turkish tradition. The crescent can be made of cardboard or plywood, the moon from a styrofoam ball, tennis ball, or other spherical object, plus a funnel for the top, a can for the bottom, and many bells of all types. Attach these as shown in the photograph and you've made the ultimate rattle.

46 Dancing Bells

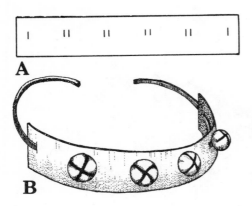

Bells are used by many cultures (American Indians, for example) to enhance the rhythmic beat of their dance. Gather four or five small spherical Christmas-type bells and a leather strip about 2" by 6" long. You will also need a leather lace or string and a sharp knife.

For each bell make one pair of slits spaced evenly across the leather strip with *one* slit at each end (A). Thread the lace or string through the end slit and through the first of the slit pairs. Thread bell onto lace and pull the lace through the other slit. Repeat. Leave enough lace at each end to tie (B). You could also sew the bells onto an elastic band or simply thread the bells onto a leather lace and tie a single knot at each juncture as you thread each bell.

Tie the finished product around your wrist, ankle, knee, or simply hold it and shake rhythmically.

Water Bells

Water bells are fun to play and easy to assemble from glasses and jars of many sizes (the finer the glass, the nicer the tone). All you need are some wooden strikers and water to put in the glass containers.

Strike each glass and select the ones that have the most pleasant sound. Vary the pitch by adding different amounts of water in each glass. To make a scale, start with an empty glass and work up the scale note by note. Thin-walled and crystal glasses have particularly pleasant tones. Songs and scales can be worked out with the same or different sizes of containers. Try soft and hard mallets for striking.

Note On fine glasses, a dampened finger rubbed around the rim will create an especially intriguing sound.

Chimes

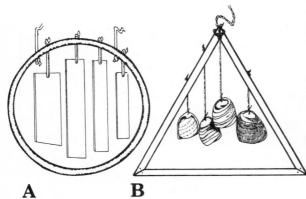

Chimes are very simple to make and can employ a wide range of materials. They can be tuned or random and can be activated either by striking or by breezes (i.e., wind chimes). The only stipulation is that they be arranged and spaced for the purpose — wind chimes close together, playing chimes separated.

Use different sizes of nails (larger ones usually have more ring), tin can lids, pieces of glass, scraps of metal, strips of wood, pieces of bamboo, segments of metal tubing, small sea shells, pieces of plastic or keys.

Chimes may be suspended from nylon line on a straight bar or, for more collisions, from a round (A) or triangular frame (B) fashioned from wood or metal stripping.

MATERIALS

Clean, unglazed, earthenware flowerpots

Heavy cord or twine

Mallet or striker

Pole or broomstick

ASSEMBLY

1. If you want a set of bells to play a scale or tonal pattern, you will have to hand-pick several sizes of pots and compare their relative pitches. Flowerpots of the same size can differ by one or two scale degrees. Size and *thickness* determine the pitch.

2. Suspend the pots upside down from a cord attached to a broomstick or other framework. Don't strike them too hard.

OPTIONS

You may either tie a large knot in the cord and insert it through the hole in each pot before tying it to the pole (A), or if the cord is too thin for a good-sized knot, tie it to a small (2") section of dowel before threading through the pot hole (B).

PLAY SUGGESTIONS

The best tone will result if hard mallets are used, though care must be taken not to strike the pot too hard, as they are relatively fragile. Make your own scale arrangements.

A

B

Tubular Bells

MATERIALS

Two 10' segments of 1/2" diameter electrical conduit tubing.

Note Different types of metal tubing have different sound characteristics. Some experimentation would be worthwhile before making too large an investment in one kind. Try stainless steel, copper, aluminum, or brass.

String

Tape or drill with high-speed bit to attach string

Dowel or stick for suspending tubes

TOOLS

Hacksaw or tube cutter

Drill with high-speed bits or strong tape

Metal file

ASSEMBLY

1. Cut the tubing to the specified lengths (A).

2. Tape string or wire about 1" from the end of each tube (or drill a hole in the tube through which the string can loop) (B).

3. Test the pitches of your scale with a striker of wood or metal.

4. Tune the pitch where necessary. It is only possible to make the pitch of the pipes higher by trimming off a bit of length, or filing patiently. If the pitch is too high, you'll have to cut another slightly longer piece. The scale diagrammed should be approximate to a D major scale.

Note Chimes may also be made from small size tubing and shorter lengths. Aluminum angle is a good alternative material for chimes. Search the room for different ways to suspend the chimes. Just make sure they are at a convenient playing height.

A

B

Tone Box

This instrument is based on an ancient Aztec drum used in initiation rites and ceremonies. The instrument may be found in a wide spectrum of sizes. It may also be called a tongue drum.

MATERIALS

Two slabs of softwood or hardwood, 1/4" thick. Wooden roofing shingles have been used with success. A hardwood top will produce a sharper tone than softwood which produces a mellow less resonant sound. The larger the sound-box, the more resonant the tone and more definite the pitch. Tone depends also on thickness and length of tongues. Use thicker tops for larger boxes.

1/2" stock for sides of sound-box

Glue

1" finishing nails or clamps, rubber bands, and weights

TOOLS

Saw

Keyhole saw or jigsaw

Drill with a 1/4" bit

Hammer, if nails are used

Finishing materials

ASSEMBLY

1. Cut wood to be used for the sides to desired lengths (A).

2. Glue and nail (or clamp) sides to the bottom slab (B) being careful to get a tight and solid fit since the instrument will be struck with mallets. Let dry.

3. The top may be glued onto the box at this point and then tongues cut (B) (this procedure is best if you want to tune each tongue as you cut) or the tongues may be cut first then glued to the sound-box.

4. On the top piece of wood, drill a row of 1/4" holes across the top about 1" in from the edge, leaving about 1" between holes (C). Arrange the holes so as to result in three tongues on each end (though more or less tongues may be desirable).

5. Repeat this process across the opposite edge.

6. Using a keyhole saw or jigsaw, join the holes opposite each other with a saw cut (C).

7. Then create a series of "H's" or tongues of wood by cutting at right angles to the previous cuts (D). The resulting tongues should be of unequal lengths for different tones.

8. Glue top to sound-box if this has not been done previously, making sure to get a good tight bond since the instrument will be struck.

9. Sand off excess edges and round the corners.

10. Finish with varnish, oil, or lacquer (follow the directions on the can).

11. Make mallets (see "Mallets" p. 62).

Note If you put wooden or rubber feet (thumbtacks partway in will do) onto the bottom of each corner of the box, this will raise the box off the table and create a richer tone. It will resonate even more if you hold it lightly in the air.

PLAYING SUGGESTIONS

Strike with hard mallets and soft mallets to get the desired effect. Strike the tongues in different places to find the "live" or most resonant spot. Mark these spots if you wish. Play rhythmic patterns over and over again creating a hypnotic effect. Change the speed and pattern according to your feelings.

Note On larger hardwood tone boxes care might be taken through experimentation to cut each tongue to a pitch. Simple rhythm boxes might consist of a soft or hardwood box with a pattern cut into each facet (E).

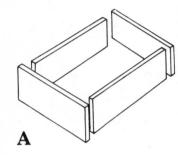

A

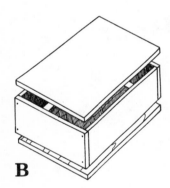

B

C

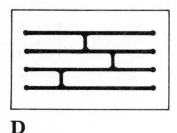

D

E

Wooden chimes make a fine resonant sound that can contribute to many musical experiences. Some care is needed in the assembly to ensure a good scale but the fun of playing is worth the extra effort.

MATERIALS
A 1" x 2" about 12' long piece of knotless softwood or hardwood. (Usually the harder the wood the more resonant the sound.)

6' of heavy baling twine

Wooden striker (dowel works fine)

Staples (optional)

TOOLS
Saw

Stapler

ASSEMBLY
1. Measure the wood and mark off the following lengths:

20"	16-1/2"
19"	15-1/2"
18"	14-1/2"
17-1/2"	13-1/2"

Note The saw cut may change your measurement slightly, so measure the next piece anew after each cut.

2. Lay the bars out from longest to shortest on a length of twine which has been laid out in a "U" shape (A). This is a convenient way to arrange the bars for testing; they will require some fine adjustment to play a proper scale.

Note Because of the particular vibration pattern of wooden bars, the twine should touch the bars about one quarter of the way in from each end. This is called a "nodal point" or a "dead spot" and will allow the rest of the bar to vibrate more freely.

3. Tap the longest bar until you can discern a clear pitch. You will probably have to be in a very quiet place and listen carefully to focus on the actual pitch.

4. Tune the next longest bar to the second scale degree.

5. Saw a little bit off the end to make the sound a little higher (B). To make the sound lower, saw a little way into the bar at the midpoint (C). A little cutting can make a lot of difference, so proceed carefully.

6. Continue with each piece until the entire scale is in tune.

7. Stabilize the bars by untwisting the twine just enough to push the bar ends through (D). The strands of twine should encircle each bar at the nodal point (one quarter the way in from each end).

8. Tie knots at each loose end.

9. Hang this arrangement or lay it on a table.

OPTION
Another possibility is to hang each bar from its end with a screw eye and string, although this method is not as effective. Suspend bars from a broom handle in the manner of the tubular bells (E).

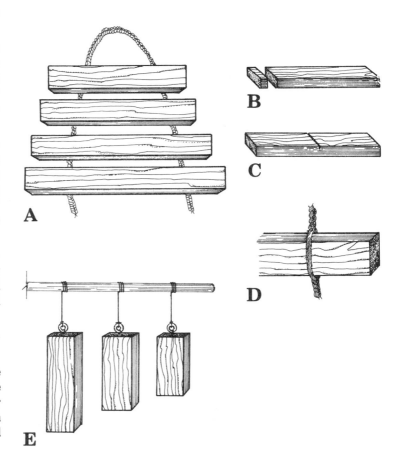

Thumb Piano

This lovely little instrument is modeled after the African kalimba which was formerly used for relaying messages during the time the slave traders assaulted the African coast. Thumb pianos are made in all shapes and sizes and are sometimes held inside a very large gourd. This enables the sound to return to the person playing the instrument.

MATERIALS

Wood strip — 24" long, 2" high, and 1/2" thick for sound-box frame

Two pieces — 7" x 5" x 1/8" plywood for top and bottom

Two strips of wood — 6-1/2" x 1/4" x 1/4" (or two 6-1/2" lengths of 1/4" doweling)

Two strips of wood — 6-1/2" x 3/4" x 3/8" (or two lengths of 3/8" doweling)

Five, eight, or more tongues of metal or wood

Use rake tines cut to 3" or 4" lengths, flattened steel or spring steel, coping saw blades cut to length, bamboo splints filed to about 1/8" thick, or popsicle sticks

3 or 4 1-1/4" screws

Finishing materials

TOOLS

Small wood saw

Hacksaw or tin snips for cutting metal tongues

Drill and bit for predrilling screw holes

Screwdriver

Small wood plane for shaping bridges

Glue and clamps or weights

ASSEMBLY

1. Saw the 24" x 2" x 1/2" strip into four pieces comprising the sides of the sound-box: two 7" lengths and two 4" lengths (A).

2. Glue and clamp side pieces to the 7" x 5" x 1/8" plywood back (B).

3. Let dry completely.

4. On the other 7" x 5" x 1/8" plywood piece, pencil the placement of bridges and sound-hole as shown (C). Leave 1/4" between bridges.

5. On the other side of the plywood (inside of box) pencil the placement of the supporting strip of wood so that when bridges and support block are glued in place they will look like the cross section drawing (E).

6. Drill sound-hole with a hole cutter or cut out by drilling a small hole through which a coping saw blade may pass (D) and reattach to the saw for careful sawing of the hole. Sand smooth. More ornate sound-holes are suggested in appendix (see p. 139).

7. Glue and clamp bridges (6-1/2" x 1/4" x 1/4") into place. Let dry.

8. Glue support strip (6-1/2" x 3/4" x 3/8") into place. Let dry.

Note If you use doweling for a support strip, flatten it on one side to increase the gluing surface to the piece of plywood.

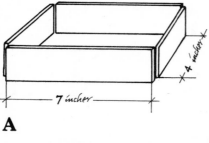

A

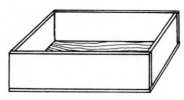

B

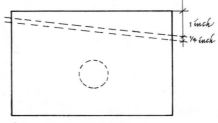

C

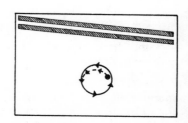

D

9. Place 6-1/2" x 3/4" x 3/8" strip between the two bridges, hold firmly, and drill pilot holes for the screws (E). The pilot holes should be just slightly smaller than the screw size. They will prevent the wood from splitting as the screws are tightened.

10. Glue the top assemblage to the sound-box, clamp, and let dry. Rubber bands or weights may be used instead of clamps.

11. Finish box with varnish, oil, or lacquer.

12. Cut tongues to length (approx. 3" to 4" for metal). Sand off all sharp edges and corners.

13. Place tongues at even intervals across box (G).

14. Carefully screw down remaining 6-1/2" x 3/4" x 3/8" strip on top of the tongues. Leave slightly loose for tuning (F).

15. Adjust the tongues to match a scale by varying the length of the vibrating portion before the screws are tightened snug.

16. If buzzes or rattles occur, check carefully the glue joints and the shaping of the bridge closest to the sound-hole. The African musician, however, would consider the buzzes and rattles a bonus. Africans often add things onto the box that will rattle to make the sound more interesting.

PLAYING SUGGESTIONS

Hold the thumb piano in both hands with thumbs plucking the tongues singly or in combinations. Pick out familiar tunes if you have the piano tuned to a regular (diatonic) scale or create your own tunings and melodies or effects.

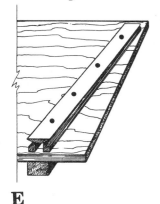

E

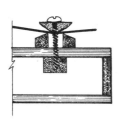

F

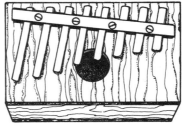

G

Wooden Xylophone

One step beyond the wooden chimes (see page 49) is the wooden xylophone which works on the same principles as the chimes but is arranged on a wooden framework for stable and convenient playing. Instruments of this sort have been found in many cultures throughout history.

MATERIALS

About 15' of clear (no knots) cedar (hardwood may also be used with excellent results). Each bar should be planed to 1-3/16" wide and 9/16" thick

5' of 1" x 3" softwood for frame stand

Glue and 1-1/2" finishing nails for assembling frame

25 — 2" finishing nails

Thick rubber bands or 4' of thin plastic tubing

Mallets (see Drumsticks and Mallets, p. 62)

TOOLS

Hammer

Plane

Drill and 1/8" bit

ASSEMBLY

1. To make frame, cut 1" x 3" stock into two 24" lengths, one 8" length, and one 4" length.

2. Glue and nail 24" runners onto the 8" and 4" pieces as shown (A).

3. Starting 1-1/2" from the end of one rail, nail the 2" finishing nails down the rail at 1-3/4" intervals.

4. Starting 2-1/2" from the end on the other rail, nail 2" finishing nails at 1-3/4" intervals. The nails are started at different intervals so that they will be juxtapositioned — one nail goes *through* each wood bar on one rail and the wood bar goes *between* the nails on the other rail (B).

5. Plane clear cedar to specified thickness and width (9/16" x 1-3/16") and cut to prescribed lengths using a saw (C). Fine tuning may be done as you cut each length (see wooden chimes for tuning techniques, p. 49).

Note If clear cedar is used in the suggested sizes, the scale will approximate an A-major scale. If hardwood is used or

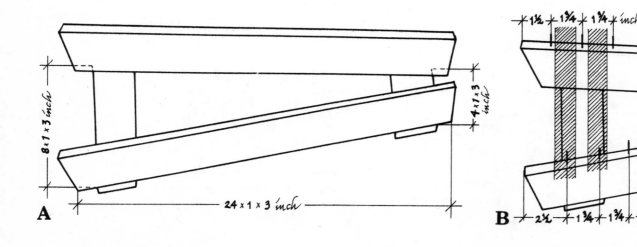

A 24 x 1 x 3 inch 8 x 1 x 3 inch 4 x 1 x 3 inch

B 1½ ¾ ¾ inch 2½ 1¾ 1¾ inch

a different width and thickness are preferred, the sound will be quite acceptable but the scale will be different. Experiment with whatever materials you have at hand.

6. Drill one 1/8" hole in each bar about one quarter of the way in from the end of each bar (D). This point should be a "nodal" point on each bar which is a point of minimal vibration thus allowing the rest of the bar to vibrate more freely. If a bar has an especially dull sound try changing its position so that the rails are touching at this nodal point. You will know because of the improved quality of tone as the bar is struck.

7. Stain and oil, lacquer, or varnish at this stage.

8. Rubber bands hitched along the nails on each rail will keep the wooden bars from touching the frame thus producing a clearer sound (E). Small diameter plastic tubing or thin sponge weather stripping glued along each rail will have the same results.

9. Hard mallets will produce a sharp clear tone.

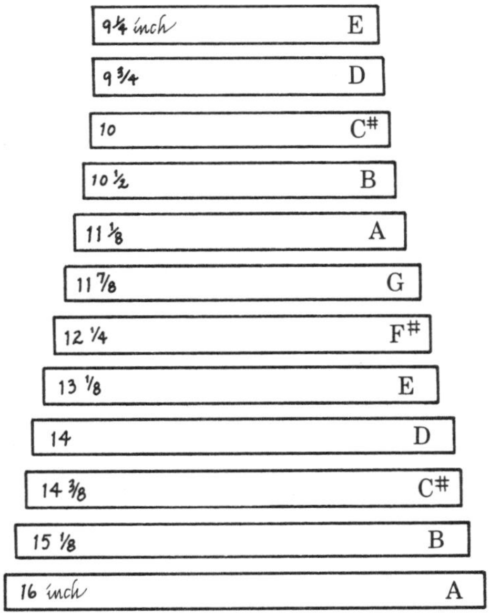

9 ¼ inch	E
9 ¾	D
10	C#
10 ½	B
11 ⅛	A
11 ⅞	G
12 ¼	F#
13 ⅛	E
14	D
14 ⅜	C#
15 ⅛	B
16 inch	A

C

D

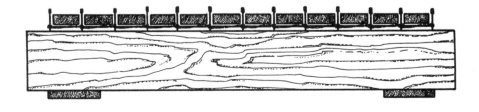

E

Tubular Glockenspiel

This beautiful sounding instrument belongs to a family of pitched percussion instruments that have a long history. The earliest xylophones, made of stone, have been found in prehistoric burial sites. Through time they made their way across cultural boundaries and are now found around the world. Glockenspiels are easy to build and are made from a variety of natural materials. These percussion sounds are very popular in some cultures. The Balinese have developed pitched percussion instruments to a high degree as evidenced by families of tuned gongs, cymbals, xylophones, and glockenspiels used in their musical expression.

MATERIALS

11' of 1/2" electrical conduit (aluminum alloy, copper, or brass)

5' of 1" x 3" softwood for frame stand

Glue and nails (1-1/2" finishing nails are best)

2' of 1/4" doweling

Long rubber bands

Mallets (see Drumsticks and Mallets, p. 62)

TOOLS

Pipe cutter or hacksaw

Saw

Hammer

Metal file

ASSEMBLY

1. To make frame, cut 1" x 3" stock into two 24" lengths, one 8" length, and one 4" length.

2. Glue and nail 24" runners onto the 8" and 4" pieces as shown (A).

3. Cut piping into prescribed lengths (B) using the pipe cutter or hacksaw. A plus or minus after the measurement points to the possible need to over or under measure by no more than 1/32". Fine tuning may be done after the glockenspiel is assembled or as you cut each length.

4. Drill 1/4" holes into top edge of runners leaving 1-3/4" between holes (C).

5. Cut doweling so that approximately 1" remains protruding from each hole. Glue dowels in holes and let dry.

6. Stain and oil, varnish, or lacquer at this stage.

7. Suspend tubes between posts by placing the end of a rubber band over an end post, twist it once, insert pipe into the rubber band, twist again and begin the process again around the next post (D).

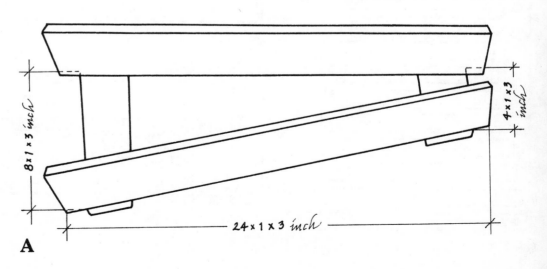

A

8 x 1 x 3 inch

4 x 1 x 3 inch

24 x 1 x 3 inch

Use several small bands if long bands are not available.

8. Repeat Step 7 along other runner. Arrange tubes so that they are graduated symmetrically (B).

9. Make soft mallets (see Drumsticks and Mallets, p. 62).

10. The pitch may be sharpened by filing a bit off the end of a pipe. However, if the pitch goes too sharp, it is best to cut a new length and use the old tube for the next highest pitch. Make sure sharp edges are filed smooth.

PLAYING SUGGESTIONS

Improvise freely or try to pick out a familiar tune using one or both mallets. Play the songs supplied in this book (see Appendix B). Experiment with different kinds of mallets. Use two, three, and four mallets simultaneously for chording. Rearrange pipes for unique tunings.

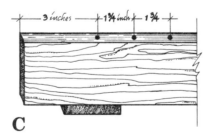

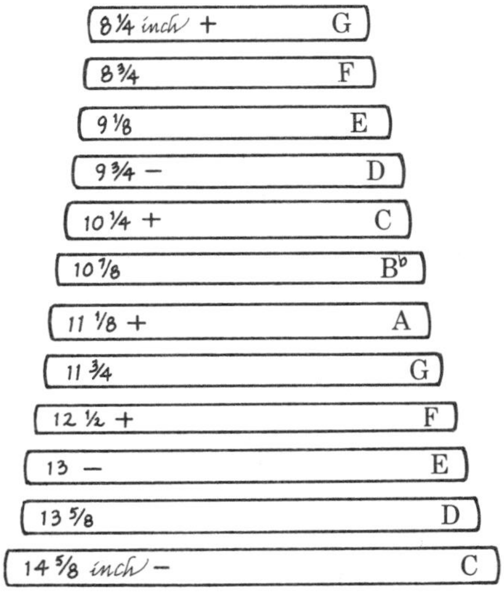

B

8 ¼ inch +	G
8 ¾	F
9 ⅛	E
9 ¾ −	D
10 ¼ +	C
10 ⅞	B♭
11 ⅛ +	A
11 ¾	G
12 ½ +	F
13 −	E
13 ⅝	D
14 ⅝ inch −	C

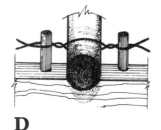

C

3 inches — 1 ¾ inch — 1 ¾

D

Drums

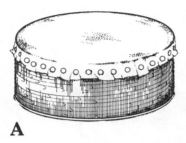

A

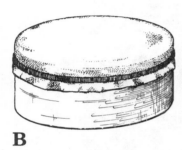

B

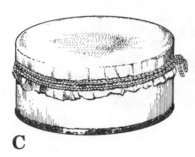

C

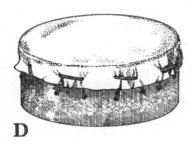

D

Drums are popular instruments that children and adults enjoy. The pleasure of playing does not require a formal instrument built to rigid specifications. Indeed, a drum can be most anything on which you can beat. The log drum of Africa and the clay-body drums of the East are two examples. Their sounds and styles contrast markedly with Western drums. What should you look for in your drum making? The only parameters for a drum are probably that it should have a moderate amount of resonance. After that you can be as inventive as you like.

Generally speaking, drums have two components: the body and the membrane. Some drums have two skins, one on top and one on bottom, but more often drums (such as the Irish bodhran and some Indian war drums) have only one skin with an open bottom. Others (like the concert kettle drums) have one skin stretched over an enclosed bowl. How you construct your drum depends on the kind of sound you want it to make. Below are listed some of the materials you might use.

Suggested materials for the body (drum frame or shell) include coffee cans, cake tins or other tins, clay pots, rigid boxes, kitchen bowls, kegs, buckets, tubs, packing cartons, and carpet tubes. **Note** Square drum frames such as those made from boxes and cartons have just as good a sound as circular drums and are often easier to work with although the round types seem to be more aesthetically pleasing to the eye.

Suggested materials for membranes or drumheads include thick paper or cardboard (sometimes used with cloth), rubber innertubes, modern vellums, cloth, rawhide, or thin plywood.

Use any of these methods to attach membranes to shell: gluing; tacking (A); jamming a hoop over the skin on to the shell (B); banding it on with twine, string, or a strand of rawhide (C); lacing it down (many different styles) (D).

HOW TO PREPARE DRUMHEADS

The following discussion describes briefly some of the common materials used for drumheads plus a few techniques used to mount them. This is followed by some specific examples of drums to build. New ideas will occur to you and you will want to experiment as you begin to build your own drum.

Materials To Use
Synthetic Vellums
Perhaps the easiest form of drumhead to work with is made from the modern synthetic materials used for snare and bass drums in contemporary bands and instrumental groups. Music stores often have broken or damaged heads that may be used for smaller folk drums. This type of membrane has the advantage of being highly resistant to weather and changes in humidity. However, some sort of tensioning mechanism is usually necessary to get the head tight enough to respond well. Drum hardware or twine and toggles work well. (See Methods for Attaching Drumheads, p. 58.)

Paper
Another form of drumhead utilizes heavy paper such as that found in grocery bags. This paper can be reinforced with cheesecloth and shellac in the following manner. The cheesecloth and paper should be layered together with the paper on the outside of the drum. Cut the layers 2" larger than the periphery of the

drum frame (A). Pass the two layers quickly under water to evenly dampen the entire surface and tie or tack them to the drum frame. You might anchor the cloth and paper temporarily with large rubber bands. Carefully pull even and tight and then tie (B). Let dry. Apply three or more coats of shellac. Let dry between coats. Do not lace paper to drum frame or it will probably tear. Tap this drum lightly; it will not stand up to hard drumming although it will produce a nice tone when tapped with the fingers.

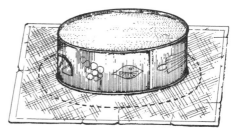

A

Cloth

Canvas, duck airplane cloth, muslin, percale, heavy linen, or modern tenting materials are suitable for cloth-faced drums. Some materials such as canvas shrink when wet. This shrinking property may be used to good advantage for construction purposes. Thoroughly dampen the material before playing to give the drum more resonance. An alternative is to coat the cloth with a few coats of airplane dope or shellac to give it resilience and body. (You should be able to find airplane dope at a hobby store or lumber store.) Pull and tack fabric on drum frame as tightly as possible before applying airplane dope or shellac.

B

Rubber

Rubber to construct a drumhead may be obtained from old innertubes. With a knife or scissors cut rubber about 1" or so larger than the drum frame (C). Pull rubber tightly and tack, lace, or band it onto the drum body. This operation may take another pair of hands to carry out successfully. If you lace the rubber onto the frame, be sure to punch lacing holes through the rubber instead of poking holes which will tear when under tension.

C

Plywood

Drums utilizing wooden tops work especially well when glued to a long narrow resonator such as a carpet tube. One-eighth inch plywood or very thin plywoods such as those used by model builders will produce a good sound and may be found at lumber stores and hobby shops. Be sure to glue the head on firmly.

Cut a variety of lengths and tie them together in a cluster or arrange in a row for a real visual and aural treat (D).

Rawhide

Untanned hide or rawhide may be bought from manufacturing outlets that deal in leather goods. (*Tanned* hides are not suitable as they will not shrink and tighten effectively after being soaked in water.) Rawhide comes in different weights or thicknesses. The hide is layered down to a specified thickness by the manufacturer. Skins for drums should be under 1/16" thick for proper tension and sound. Old tympani heads are sometimes made of natural skins. Check your local music stores, hobby shops, and stockyards for other possible sources for rawhide. Calf, lamb, or goat skin will give the best results. Cowhide is usually too thick.

D

Cut rawhide approximately 2" larger than the frame of the drum. Soak in lukewarm water for an hour or two, or soak the skin in cool water for a full day. Place the skin onto the drum frame while it is wet. *Do not* pull the hide very tight at this point. Rather, concentrate on tacking, lacing, or banding it firmly so that it is even and smooth around the head and has no wrinkles in it. Once again, do not pull skin too taut while attaching it. If the head gets too tight as it dries it may crush the drum frame or tear the skin. If extensive lacing is used, the hide

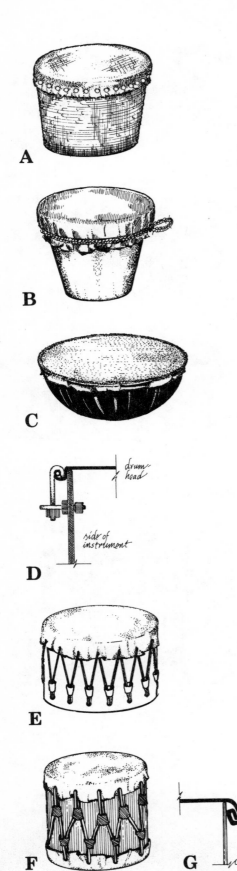

A

B

C

drum head

side of instrument

D

E

should be hand dampened every so often to maintain its elasticity. Let the skin dry slowly for a full day before attempting to play the instrument.

HOW TO MOUNT DRUMHEADS

Methods To Use

Tacking

Use short bulletin board tacks on heads which will have to be removed and replaced from time to time. This advice applies to the paper and cheesecloth drum (A). Long furniture tacks with decorative heads may be used for a more permanent arrangement.

Banding

Banding is most effective when used on a drum or vessel with a protruding lip around the edge so that the band will not slip off under tension or during playing (B). Heavy rubber bands provide good temporary banding and may be used in conjunction with twine or string for more stability. Twine, string, or strong thread may be threaded through holes punched around the skin at 1'' to 2'' intervals (C). The holes should be arranged just under the lip of the drum vessel so that when the skin tightens or when the string is secured it will pull the membrane tight. Thin strips of wet rawhide make excellent banding material because the rawhide will shrink and tighten as it dries, giving it more holding power.

Commercial Hardware

The type of hardware found on commercial drums and banjo heads with screw adjusters work the best when using synthetic drum skins (D). They are rather expensive, however, and are not in the true homemade tradition, although screw adjusters may be fashioned from scratch. (See Appendix C, Irving Sloan's book on *Making Musical Instruments*.) If screw adjusters are used the drumhead needs to be mounted on a rim or hoop for even tensioning. (See lacing instructions below.)

Lacing

An alternative to the commercial tensioning hardware is a zigzag pattern of lacing which incorporates toggles. Use a single set of lacing and toggles for a single skin (E) and a double set for a two-skin drum (F). Another tensioning trick is to add wedges or "shoes" under the lacing to pull the skin tighter.

There is nothing in particular to watch for when lacing a moderately thick membrane onto a shell. If you are careful to punch holes and use one of the appropriate lacing styles described here you will have good results. Thinner skins,

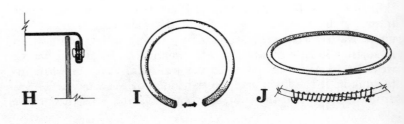

F   G   H   I   J

however, will sometimes tear as they dry or as they are played if the lacing is only threaded through a single thickness. One solution to this problem is to fold the edge of the skin over two or three times to reinforce it (G). Once the holes have been punched, grommets may be used to reinforce them and to add a decorative touch (H). Another technique used to mount thin drumskins is to bend a thin tree branch or strip of beech or willow into a hoop by soaking the branch in water and/or bending it slowly around a hot pipe (I). The hoop should be a little larger than the diameter of the drum shell. Join the ends of the wood strip with a scarf joint (J) and strap tightly or glue. With a string, thread, and needle whip the skin on to the hoop (K). Punch holes.

There is an endless variety of lacing styles. The style used is determined by the type of membrane, the shape and size of the drum shell or frame, and whether the drum has a single or double head. Below are some of the more common lacing techniques.

SINGLE HEAD

Simplest form of lacing a single skin to a shell. Punch holes into skin and an equal number of holes into shell. Lace as shown with twine or leather lacing (L).

Separate loops of lacing are entwined through holes drilled around the shell. The membrane lacing is then zigzaged as shown (M).

Lacing goes from membrane across the bottom of the drum to the opposite side and back gradually working around the circumference or may tie onto a ring of leather at bottom of the drum (N).

Methods of lacing incorporating pegs (O).

DOUBLE HEAD

A common form of "N" pattern lacing (P).

"X" lacing is a zigzag which alternates the lacing pattern into every other hole (Q).

Net lacing is a type of "N" lacing with connecting laces between zigzags (R).

Overlap skins over a thin shell and sew them together (S).

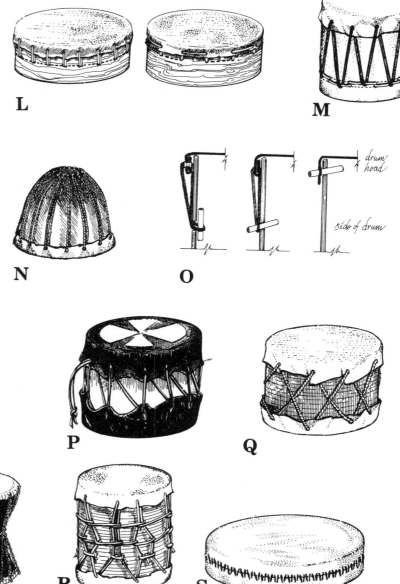

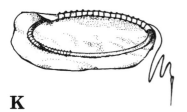

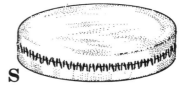

Bamboo Slit Drum

Slit drums may be found in a variety of styles and sizes. The classic talking drums of Africa are slit drums made from large logs which have been hollowed out through a long slit cut the length of the log. Each lip on either side of the slit is thinned out to varying degrees so that a difference in pitch and timbre is achieved thus producing a modulation resembling speech.

MATERIALS

A length of 1" to 2" diameter bamboo

A drill and 3/16" bit

Keyhole saw

Mallets with hard knobs

ASSEMBLY

1. Cut a length of bamboo which includes the natural nodes or joints at each end.

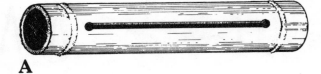

A

2. Since bamboo has such a hard enamel skin you may find it difficult to drill and saw. It is helpful to have two extra hands to secure it while doing these operations. Make sure your tools are sharp.

3. Drill two 3/16" holes about 2" from each end.

4. With the saw cut two parallel lines connecting the two holes and remove the waste (A).

5. Be careful not to split the bamboo or you will have to begin anew.

6. Experiment with slots of varying lengths and widths.

Double-Headed Tom Tom

One of the easier drums to make utilizes an innertube laced over a cake tin, can, or other hollow cylinder such as carpet tubing, large diameter pipes, or hollow logs. Its size and lightness make it a convenient instrument to carry on horseback into battle. Though rubber is used in this example, any of the suggested drumheads may be employed. Lacing is not advisable for this drum if you use cloth or paper drumskins.

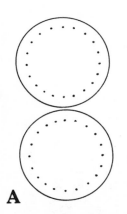

A

B

C

MATERIALS

One rubber innertube

One cake tin about 3" or 4" deep

Twine or lacing

Pencil

Scissors or utility knife

ASSEMBLY

1. Cut the bottom out of the cake tin. An electric can opener will do a neat job.

2. Hammer down any rough edges if bottom is cut out by hand. Decorate if you wish.

3. Cut open the innertube so that you have one flat length which will cover the two open sides of the cake tin.

4. Lay the tin onto the rubber tube and draw a line around it about 1" larger than the circumference of the tin.

5. Flip the tin over and make another circle. Cut both circles with scissors or knife (A).

6. Punch holes with a paper punch all around the edge (about every inch) (A). *Do not* poke holes into rubber, for the lacing, with a needle or sharp object as the rubber will tear. Holes must be punched.

7. Stretch the tubes over the tin so they meet on the sides evenly.

8. Temporarily tie this together while you begin lacing and work all the way around (B).

Note The tube should be moderately tight to give a proper tone. You will have to work your way around the drum several times tightening the lacing a little more each round.

9. Tie a good knot (C).

10. Decorate heads if you wish.

The square drum was often used by Indians of northwest coast areas because of the availability of packing crates. You will find this an easy and effective drum to make.

MATERIALS

Wooden packing crate approximately 12" x 15" x 2" or saw your own sides (white cedar was used by Indians).

1-1/2" finishing nails and hammer

Long tacks such as furniture tacks with decorative heads

Rawhide

Glue

Scissors

PROCEDURE

1. Saw two 12" lengths and two 15" lengths of wood that are about 1/2" to 1" thick. Make the frame smaller if your piece of rawhide is not large enough to accommodate the suggested size.

2. Glue and nail drum frame together (A). Let dry.

3. Soak rawhide in cool water overnight or in lukewarm water for an hour or two.

4. Trim rawhide to shape so that both sides will be covered with enough to wrap around and tack.

5. Tack rawhide to one side of frame, then pull skin around the box so that skin overlaps the sides and is reasonably taut, not tight. Place a tack about every inch (B).

6. Repeat on the other side. Tack skin along edges. Cut out corners so skin will lay flat (C).

7. Let dry slowly overnight.

8. Decorate.

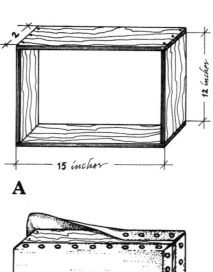

A

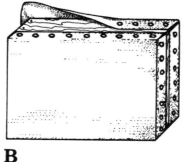

B

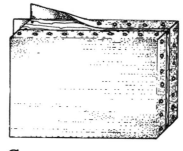

C

Drumsticks and Mallets

These sticks and mallets may be used on many percussion instruments. It is important that the mallet be matched to the instrument so that it will feel "right" in the hand and give the desired sound.

MATERIALS
Sticks
1/4" to 1/2" doweling from 8" to 12" long

Chopsticks

Tree stems

PROCEDURE
Hard Ends
Take about a foot of 1/2" doweling and carve a broad groove about 5/8" from the end. Sand the ends round, wax (A).

Wooden beads drilled out to fit a 1/4" dowel or stick and glued together make good hard mallets (B).

Cork that is carved in a round shape or old cork fishing floats fitted to a dowel or stick are also fine beaters.

Plastic balls or spools may be glued to a stick.

Soft Ends
On about one foot of doweling wrap and wind yarn or jute twine as tight as possible until it reaches a diameter of approximately 1". Dab the yarn end completely with white glue. Hold for a few minutes and let dry thoroughly before using (C) (D).

Wind a strip of felt around the end of a dowel dabbing a bit of white glue as you wrap.

Small rubber balls or erasers carved a round shape and drilled out to fit on the end of a thin dowel make good beaters.

Cork, plastic, or wooden balls glued on a dowel and covered with felt, fur, leather, yarn, or other cloth material (such as wool) are excellent (E). The covering may be either glued onto the core or wrapped around tightly and tied just under the knob with string or lacing (F).

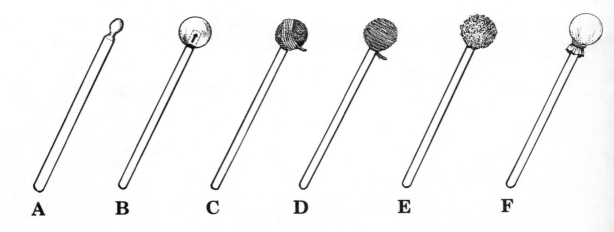

A   **B**   **C**   **D**   **E**   **F**

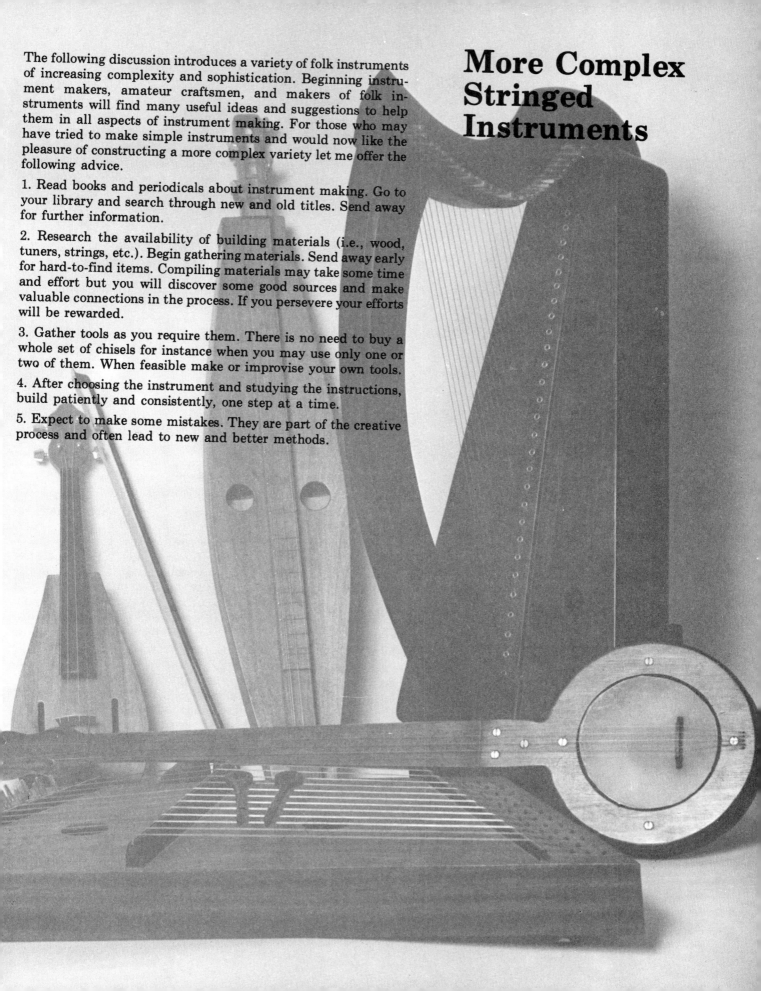

The following discussion introduces a variety of folk instruments of increasing complexity and sophistication. Beginning instrument makers, amateur craftsmen, and makers of folk instruments will find many useful ideas and suggestions to help them in all aspects of instrument making. For those who may have tried to make simple instruments and would now like the pleasure of constructing a more complex variety let me offer the following advice.

1. Read books and periodicals about instrument making. Go to your library and search through new and old titles. Send away for further information.

2. Research the availability of building materials (i.e., wood, tuners, strings, etc.). Begin gathering materials. Send away early for hard-to-find items. Compiling materials may take some time and effort but you will discover some good sources and make valuable connections in the process. If you persevere your efforts will be rewarded.

3. Gather tools as you require them. There is no need to buy a whole set of chisels for instance when you may use only one or two of them. When feasible make or improvise your own tools.

4. After choosing the instrument and studying the instructions, build patiently and consistently, one step at a time.

5. Expect to make some mistakes. They are part of the creative process and often lead to new and better methods.

More Complex Stringed Instruments

WOODS FOR STRINGED INSTRUMENTS

Softwoods and the Soundboard

The soundboard (also called the top or face) of stringed instruments is the most important area in determining the final sound. Traditionally, German spruce has always been held in high regard for constructing the soundboard and the best violin makers would choose only the wood growing between the trunk and first limbs on the south side of a tree which was growing on the south side of a mountain and cut it only in the depths of winter when the sap was down. The drying process was also important and it was years and even decades before the wood was deemed useful.

Thankfully today we need not go through such an arduous process, although there are a few basic rules to keep in mind when selecting wood. As well as German spruce there are a number of North American softwoods that have proven to be of excellent quality. For example, western red cedar, Canadian yellow cedar and sitka spruce are used by major guitar companies everywhere and should be available through most lumber stores.

Grain Configurations

The best soundboard wood has a grain configuration of long straight parallel lines with minimal defects on the face and an end grain of vertical annual rings (A). Wood cut in this manner is not only strong and stable but also conducts vibrations readily the full length of the top. This configuration is the result of a quarter cut log whereby a log is split (quartered) with a froe, dried, and further cut for the designated instrument (B).

Cutting a log or billet from the tree is a task that is usually reserved for the die-hard luthier or traditionally minded woodsman. However, long drying time (two to five years) makes this method rather inefficient for most craftsmen. One alternative to quartering your own log is to search through a stack of spruce or cedar at your local lumberyard and examine the face and end grain carefully for the vertical grain pattern. Most wood cut in modern mills is passed through a saw so that the resulting grain pattern is whorled or irregular and the end grain passes from edge to edge rather than from face to face (C). The wood has been slab cut from a log (D) so that in an entire log there will be one or two planks in the center that will yield the vertical pattern desirable for instrument tops (E). A thorough search through a pile of slab-cut softwood will usually turn up two or three quartered planks. If you get on good terms with the lumberyard foreman and explain to him what you are doing he can be of invaluable help to you in finding just the right material. Remember to restack lumber piles neatly so that you won't be viewed as a nuisance at any yard.

The next step is to check your plank visually (take a little plane if the lumber is rough) and then chip two corners off and see how they break. A clean chip indicates a slash grain and such wood is not desirable but a straight chip and break shows a straight-grained wood suitable for instruments (F). This step is not an absolute necessity but it should be developed by the more decerning maker.

A

B

C

D   E

Another advantage of most wood in commercial lumberyards is that it has already been dried in large kilns to a degree of usability. Nevertheless, be sure to inquire about how the wood has been dried and what moisture content to expect. After buying lumber I usually let it condition in my workshop for a period of time before I begin resawing. After each main component has been cut from a plank, I stack the pieces with strips of wood between them so that air may circulate around each piece. The wood will then continue to "cure" until the time comes to use it.

Plywood

Another alternative for soundboard wood is a thin high-grade plywood. Some Japanese and North American guitars are now being made from plywood with a great degree of success. The advantage of plywood is that it is usually impervious to warpage, is stable and strong, and is available in wide widths that don't have to be resawn from a plank into thin slabs.

The best plywood for plucked stringed instruments is used in aviation projects and was formerly found exclusively in old airplanes. Today such wood is most often imported from European sources and consists of three plys of very thin wood veneer glued together resulting in a 3/32" thickness. Such plywood is now difficult to find but your local hobby shops and aviation clubs may be of assistance. Another type of plywood that can be used effectively consists of a 1/8" 3-layer sandwich with a good hardwood of birch or mahogany on the outside faces. Perhaps the most readily available plywood that would be adequate for your building purposes if the other plywoods are not available is a 1/8" 3-layer plywood with a good layer of hardwood on one side and a lesser grade of wood on the back and in the middle.

Note I have had excellent results using plywood to build folk instruments and have found it most useful in situations where power tools were not available for slicing thin plates of wood from solid stock. Because of its efficiency and availability, I have used plywood for the construction of most of the instruments in this book. However, solid stock wood may be substituted wherever desired.

Resawing

A band saw is the most efficient tool for resawing. If you do not have access to a band saw I would suggest that you buy wood already resawn from a luthier supply house. Alternatively, you may be able to find a shop or mill that will do the sawing for you.

In order to resaw you will need to set up a guide wall parallel with the blade to hold the wood straight. A 2 x 8 or other stable invention will work well. Use a *new* 1/2" skiptooth blade. Dull blades with a worn set to the teeth will bind and wander ruining your efforts. Make sure the guide wall and blade are at a perfect right angle to the band saw table. Practise on a wood scrap to make sure it is cutting the proper thickness (depending on the type of instrument you are making). Push the wood through very *slowly*, keeping pressure against the guide wall. At the end pull it through with equal concentration. Then sand or plane to final thickness.

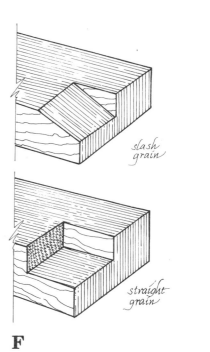

slash grain

straight grain

F

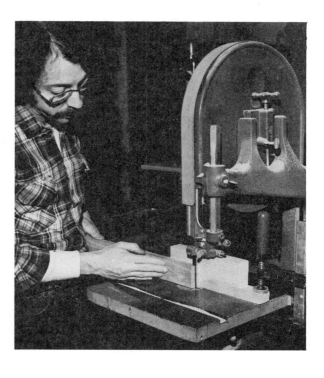

Hardwoods and the Sound-box

The back, sides, and neck of almost all stringed instruments are made of hardwood. The most sought after of these woods is Brazilian rosewood. It is favored by professional luthiers for most fretted instruments because of its hardness and beautiful deep red colors. The traditional standard material for the violin family is flamed or curly maple which has an unusual undulating grain of great beauty. Both rosewood and figured maple are expensive and they are difficult woods to work thus are not recommended for the novice. Beginning makers will find that almost any hardwood will suffice for most folk instruments. However, mahogany and walnut are the best woods for general use, while oak is rarely used because of its open grain and tendency to develop checks and cracks. Sycamore, poplar, maple, cherry, beech, and birch can also be used but each has its own idiosyncracies which are best experienced by working with the wood. Descriptive books are available that illustrate wood characteristics. Before you begin your plan consult your local hardwood dealers to find what wood is most available in your area and ask woodworkers about wood characteristics and experiment with scrap samples of each type. Each instrument has its own requirements which sometimes utilize special types of wood for certain parts. These will be mentioned in the instructions for individual projects.

Quarter-sawn material is preferable for the back and sides of a stringed instrument because of its stability and resistance to atmospheric changes. Unfortunately such material is extremely difficult to find because the milling procedures used today yield wood mostly cut on the slab. However, slab-cut back and sides work quite well for most projects as long as the wood has been properly seasoned to guard against a high shrinkage factor.

Hardwoods and the Neck

Necks also demand special care. They must be quarter sawn because of the amount of tension applied by the strings. The wood is much stronger and less likely to flex under tension when arranged as shown in (G). This can usually be achieved by turning a slab-cut plank on edge so the grain will then take on a vertical configuration (H).

Humidity

The humidity factor is an important consideration in the making of instruments. The main points to watch are the following.

1. Wood expands when humidity is high and shrinks when humidity is low.

2. 50 per cent humidity is a good working atmosphere.

3. It is better to work in a dry atmosphere than in a damp one. A completed piece will swell without harm but shrinkage of a piece may result in separations and cracks. Never glue or laminate on a rainy day.

4. It is best to do your building in hot-dry or cold-freezing weather and not in a hot and humid climate.

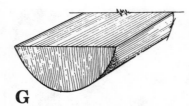

G

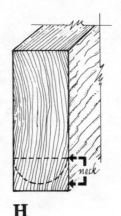

neck

H

TOOLS

There are some instruments that require very few tools for their proper construction. Others are more complicated and for them a speciality or power tool is recommended. The main tools needed to build the instruments in this book are common woodworking implements which are available at hardware stores. Some tools may even be made from scratch or improvised for a special situation. If you have some basic tools you will find that you can build most instruments with a limited range of extra equipment.

Saws

I recommend two types of saws — one to cut straight lines and one that can cut curved lines. In the first case a sharp hand saw and a little practise will reap good results. If you have access to a shop with power tools, a table saw, radial arm saw, or band saw will also cut straight lines accurately. Skill saws and jigsaws, although not as easy to control, may also be useful for this operation.

Curved or irregular cuts may be executed with a coping saw or fret saw (this is especially useful for ornate sound-holes). Use band saws and jigsaws for ornate cutting, shaping scrolls, and ornate peg heads as well as for cutting smaller pieces of wood. I have found that a dovetail saw is also useful for cutting smaller pieces of wood.

Drills

A hand twist drill, brace and bit, power hand drill, or drill press are all good tools for making accurate holes. You will find them useful for round sound-holes and tuning mechanism holes. The size of the hole may dictate which tool to use.

Planes

Hand planes, a power press plane, or a jointer can thin wood and smooth surfaces to accurate measurements. Scrapers and sandpaper are also useful for smoothing when there is not too much wood to remove.

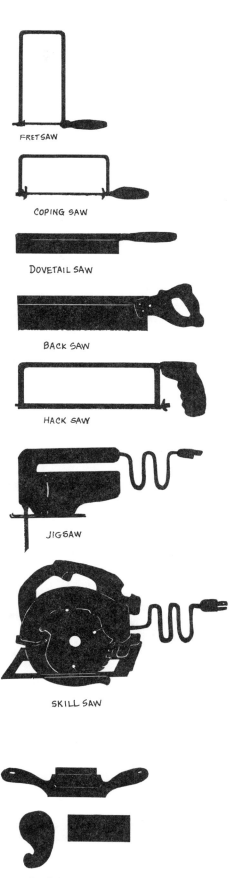

FRET SAW

COPING SAW

DOVETAIL SAW

BACK SAW

HACK SAW

JIGSAW

SKILL SAW

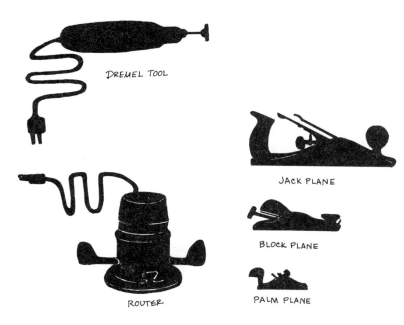

DREMEL TOOL

JACK PLANE

BLOCK PLANE

PALM PLANE

ROUTER

TOP- CABINET SCRAPER
BOTTOM - HAND SCRAPERS

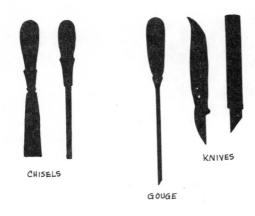

CHISELS

KNIVES

GOUGE

REAMER

FILES

RATTAIL FILE

Knives and Files

Sharp knives, one or two chisels, and a mallet are useful for removing small areas of wood. Files may serve the same purpose.

Note   All tools *must* be sharp (see Appendix A for further information).

Be patient when learning to use a tool.

Clamps

Clamps are excellent devices to make gluing and laminating easier and more effective. As you build you can assemble your own collection of clamps depending on your needs. As well, large rubber bands or pieces of elastic are useful. Often large bricks or stones or steel objects can take the place of clamps. Always clamp or weight pieces first *without* glue to check for a good joint — then apply the glue and clamp. The more clamps the more even the hold.

Vise

The bench vise is useful for holding your work stable while you are working on it. There are several different styles and sizes available from your local hardware store.

Glues

Any modern wood glue will give you good service.

White glues seem to be preferred by most woodworkers because these glues have a medium drying time and they dry clear. Some brands dry harder than others.

Hide glue dries very slowly thus allowing for the positioning of difficult parts. I find this an excellent glue.

The cream-colored *aliphatic glues* dry fast and hold well.

Epoxy glues can be used in special instances where an extra strong bond is desired. They come in fast- and slow-drying varieties.

Note   Never use rubber cement for laminating. (It is useful only in veneering.) Never use "Krazy Glue."

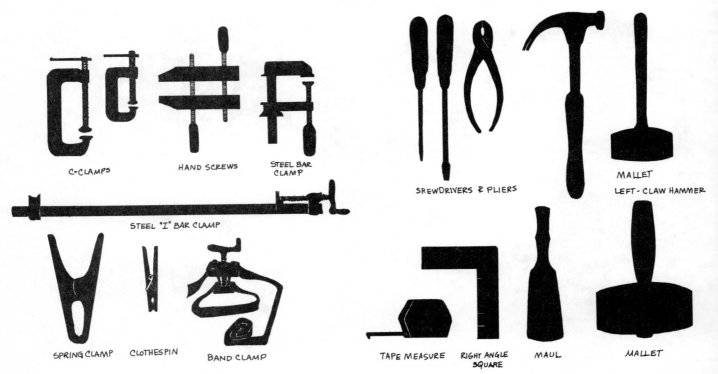

C-CLAMPS

HAND SCREWS

STEEL BAR CLAMP

STEEL "I" BAR CLAMP

SPRING CLAMP   CLOTHESPIN

BAND CLAMP

SREWDRIVERS & PLIERS

MALLET

LEFT-CLAW HAMMER

TAPE MEASURE   RIGHT ANGLE SQUARE   MAUL   MALLET

TUNING SUGGESTIONS

If you have never tuned a stringed instrument before, I would suggest you find someone who has had some previous experience. Possibly a musician friend could help you. Tuning an instrument may be one of the most difficult steps you will encounter in learning to play your new instrument. But it is the first step so you must master it. I have included some instructions on basic tunings for each instrument with the building directions; as well there are many books available to instruct you in other tunings as your skills improve.

In order to make the best sound, your instrument needs to be fine tuned. In spite of the fact that many old handcrafted instruments are notoriously out of tune and therein lies some of their charm, you should still attempt to train your ear and tuning technique to get a true sound. To do this, patience is the rule. You will need a piano, pitch pipe, or harmonica to help get your tuning technique started. Tune the instrument as closely as you can to the designated notes, then go over the instrument again to fine tune it. If the instrument is newly made it may take a period of time for it to "settle" before the strings will stabilize (especially the hammered dulcimer and harp). Because of this frequent tuning sessions will be necessary. Tuning takes patience even for the best musicians. Your ear will improve and become more discriminating the more you tune.

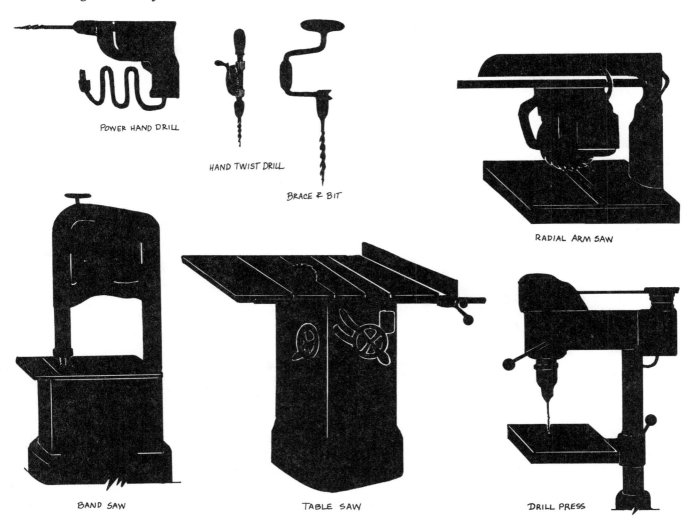

POWER HAND DRILL

HAND TWIST DRILL

BRACE & BIT

RADIAL ARM SAW

BAND SAW

TABLE SAW

DRILL PRESS

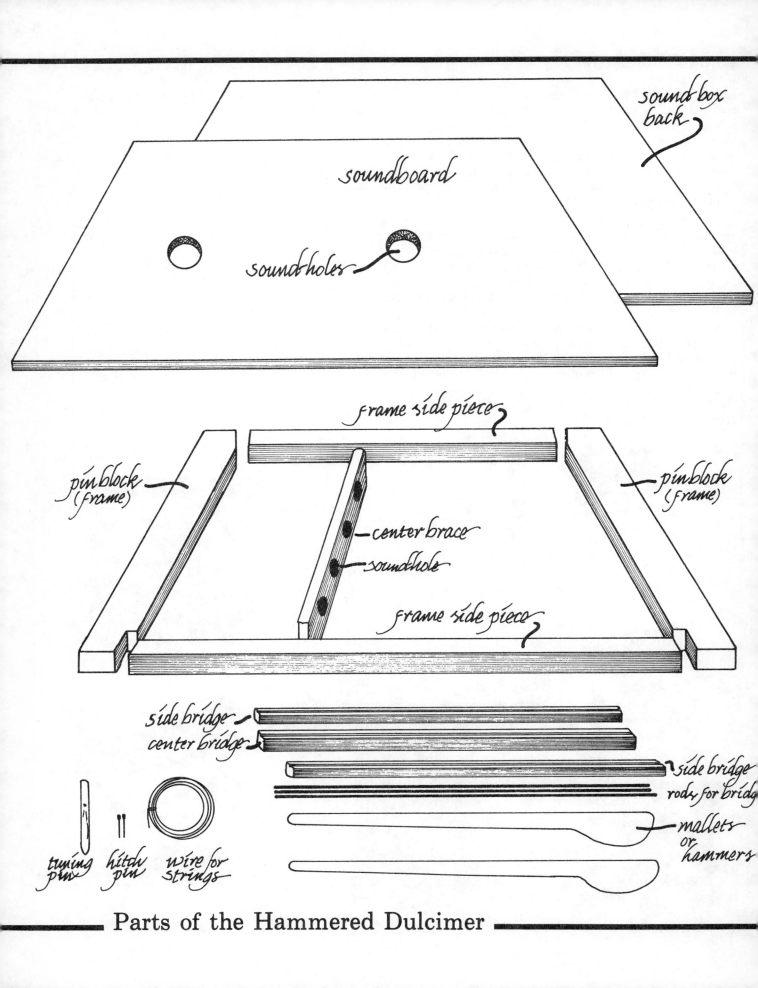

sound box
back

soundboard

sound holes

frame side piece

pin block
(frame)

pin block
(frame)

center brace

soundhole

frame side piece

side bridge

center bridge

side bridge

rods for bridg

mallets
or
hammers

tuning
pin

hitch
pin

wire for
strings

Parts of the Hammered Dulcimer

The hammered dulcimer is one of the more ancient forms of stringed instruments. Historians suggest that it originated over 5,000 years ago in Near Eastern regions where it was called the santir and psanterim. From there it spread east and west where it found popularity in such diverse cultures as Spain, England, China, India, and Europe. It wasn't until the eighteenth and nineteenth centuries that English colonists introduced it into the United States. It is still referred to as a "lumberjack piano" in some northern regions of the States because of its resemblance in character to the modern piano.

Perhaps the dulcimer found its highest refinement in the Hungarian cimbalom which is a floor standing instrument that has a chromatic range of four octaves and a damping mechanism. Most hammered dulcimers have a two- to three-octave range capable of playing diatonically in three or four keys. The unique placement of bridges on those that have a set of bass strings has increased the range and versatility of the instrument without increasing the size. As with all folk-oriented instruments the dulcimer is found in a wide range of sizes and shapes although most instruments form a trapezodial shape and are designed to sit on a table or holding stand while being played with two small hammers or mallets.

The hammered dulcimer should not be confused with the plucked Appalachian Mountain dulcimer whose name was probably borrowed from the hammered variety by early settlers in the eastern United States. The plucked dulcimer relies on frets for pitch diversity whereas the hammered dulcimer has a different string for each pitch. The name dulcimer, incidentally, means "sweet sound."

Note The dulcimer described here features a single treble bridge with three strings per course or pitch. If you wish to build a dulcimer with two bridges, the introduction of the second bridge greatly increases the amount of work involved. After experimenting with the single bridge variety those who wish to proceed with the double bridge chord should consult Appendix A of this book.

MATERIALS

3/4" plywood or hardwood back

1/4" high-grade plywood or spruce (cedar or redwood) top

2" thick maple plank or other hardwood

1" thick maple plank or other hardwood

ASSEMBLY
Sound-box
Back

1. Cut the back of the dulcimer from the 3/4" stock to the dimensions shown (A).

Note If you decide to use hardwood for the back you will probably have to laminate two pieces edge to edge to achieve the necessary dimensions. Hardwood acts as a slightly better sound reflecting surface than plywood. Consult an elementary woodworking book for laminating techniques.

Sides and Pinblocks

2. The stock for the pinblocks and sides should be planed smooth to a thickness of 2" and sawn to a width of 3-1/4". Maple is suggested because of its hard-

ness and its ability to hold the great tension on the tuning pins. Maple, however, is a difficult wood to work and must be approached with sharp tools (see Tool Sharpening Appendix A). Softer hardwoods such as basswood, cherry, poplar, and sycamore may be used and even softwoods will work if large piano pins are used instead of the smaller zither pins. Softwood, however, is suggested only if other woods are not available.

3. Lay pinblock stock on the back piece of wood and draw lines at each end to deliniate the length of each block. Cut one for each side (1) (B).

4. From the 1" thick hardwood plank (which may be resawn from the 2" thick stock on a table saw if you wish) cut the two remaining components of the frame so that they measure approximately 1" x 2" and fit between the two pinblocks.

5. Cut notches on each pinblock as shown using the band saw or a sharp hand saw (C). The 1" x 2" pieces should fit snugly into the notches to help stabilize the frame against shifting when the great string pressure is exerted (2).

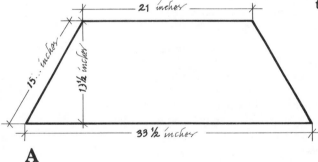

A

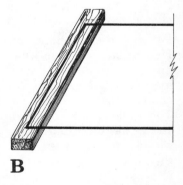

B

1 *Lay pinblock stock on back piece and draw lines to delineate length of each block*

2 *Pinblock and side junction*

6. Glue the pinblocks to the back. If you don't have clamps use heavy weights or 1-1/2" finishing nails nailed through the back. It is usually advisable to spread a thin layer of glue on both gluing surfaces. Do not try to glue too much at once. Use the 1" x 2" pieces as spacers while weighting or clamping the pinblocks, then after they dry, fit and glue the 1" x 2" pieces in place. If you feel confident, it can all be done at once as shown in photograph (3).

7. Trim excess from around edges of frame on the jointer or with a sharp hand plane.

Center Brace

8. At this point if the box does not conform to the suggested dimensions you will have to do some figuring to determine the exact placement of the center brace. It is important that it be glued in the box at a ratio of 2:3 from the sides of the instrument (D). A pocket calculator makes the measurement easy to check. Fashion a brace 3/4" wide and the same height as the frame components. Drill large holes through the brace to connect the two sound chambers (4). Glue in place and clamp or weight (5).

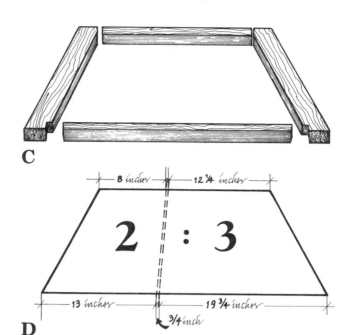

C

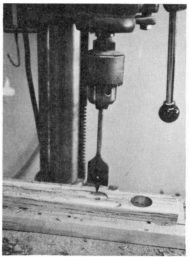

D

3 *Glue and clamp pinblock and sides to back*

4 *Drill holes in center brace*

5 *Glue and clamp center brace in place*

Soundboard

9. Cut the 1/4" plywood stock to the same dimension as your frame size (6). Set this aside for the moment.

Bridges

10. Wood molding may be used for the two side bridges or they may be fashioned from the maple or hardwood left over from the other components (E). The molding or hardwood strip should have a groove or hollow along its length into which rests a small steel rod or wire (coathanger) to support the strings. This will give the instrument a better sound and prevent the strings from cutting into the wood. A Dremel tool with a small round bit is used here to cut this groove (7). The groove may also be cut with a knife if you are careful. It may be easier to cap the top of all the bridges with a folded strip of tin or copper (F). Cut the bridges to length.

11. The center bridge should be shaped from hardwood material and also grooved or capped to keep the strings from cutting the wood (G).

Sound-holes

12. Mock up the instrument by placing the soundboard on the frame or sound-box and position the side bridges so that they rest on the edges of the pinblocks which should be 3" from the outside edge (8). The center bridge should be positioned so that it is right above the center brace.

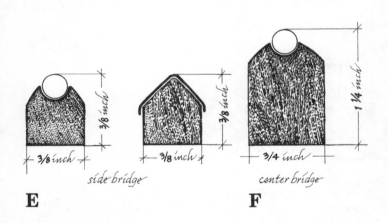

E F

7 *Cut groove in bridges with Dremel tool*

6 *Soundboard preparation*

8 *Measure side bridge placement*

Center a sound-hole in each of the two areas delineated by the bridges. Circular holes carefully drilled are the easiest although you may saw them with a fret saw if you wish (9). The example in photograph (10) has 2" sound-holes. Heart-shaped holes are the most traditional. If more ornate sound-holes are decided upon, I suggest making a pattern of them on heavy paper first, cutting them out and tracing the shape lightly onto the soundboard. Stand back and double check their placement. Drill out all areas possible. Shape further with a sharp knife, fret saw, files, and sandpaper.

Top Assembly

13. Place the top onto the sound-box and check the contact of the two parts. You may have to sand or file the sound-box frame so that it is perfectly level and flat. Next, spread a layer of glue on all parts that will contact the top or soundboard. Place top onto the sound-box, position, and clamp (10). Large rubber bands or weights may be used if you don't have enough clamps. The more weights you use and the more even distribution of their pressure the better. Let dry completely. File and sand excess around edges after glue has set.

14. Mark the placement of the bridges on the top. Glue and clamp or weight the two side bridges but do not glue the center bridge so that accurate tuning adjustments may be made as you string it up. Again, the string length of the two sides of strings between the side bridges and center bridge should be in a 2:3 ratio which will produce the musical interval of a sol-do or perfect fifth relationship. This means that there will be a five note difference between the right and left side of the center bridge on each string. Double check your measurements. The string pressure will hold the center bridge in place.

Tuning pins

15. Piano tuning pins or zither pins come in a range of sizes any of which will suffice for the hammered dulcimer. A piano store might even have used pins that will look fine when you shine them up and have the added advantage of being less expensive. Make sure, however, that you can get a tuning wrench for the size of pin that you buy. Piano wrenches are more expensive than the zither pin wrench that is used for the autoharp. The wrench, in fact, may be the most expensive item of the instrument construction. If wrench cost is prohibitive I have found that a clock key may sometimes be used instead. It is crucial that the holes for the pins be drilled just a tiny bit smaller so that the pins will hold firmly. But at the same time they should not be too tight. Make sure you test first

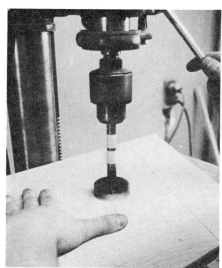

9 *Drill sound-holes*

10 *Glue and clamp soundboard*

on a scrap piece of hardwood. The hitch pins (opposite the tuning pins) may be 1" or 1-1/2" finishing nails or piano bridge pins. For best results predrill before hammering them in.

Pin Pattern

16. There are twelve courses of three strings each which means each note has three strings. The pins should be arranged in the following manner (H). First plan the pin placement. It is best to work with a long ruler on a pinblock-sized piece of paper which will give you an actual size pattern from which to work. After making the pattern for one side simply flip the pattern over for the other side. The strings in each course should be grouped closely but not so closely that they bump the next tuning pin.

After your pattern has been made and marked onto the instrument (11) double

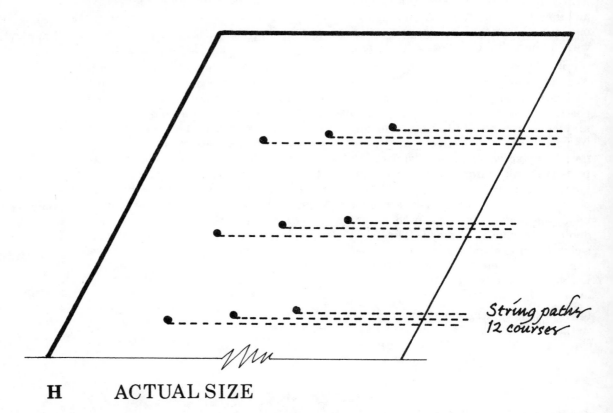

String paths 12 courses

H   **ACTUAL SIZE**

I

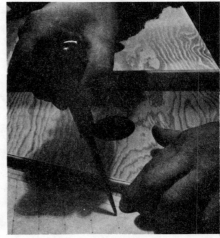

11 *Transfer tuning pin pattern*

check your string paths with a ruler (which tuning pin matches which hitch pin), then drill the holes for the tuning and hitch pins. Drilling the holes at a slight angle will help keep the string down toward the base of the pin and insure a clean "break" as the string passes over the bridge (I).

Case

17. An optional step at this point is to glue or nail the side panels around the instrument to add a more craftsman-like touch (J). Any hardwood or softwood will do. An easier alternative, as in photo (12), is to veneer the sides of the instrument using available veneers, a sharp knife, and contact cement. Read the directions on the can or consult a beginner's woodworking book for the method.

Finishing

18. Stain the instrument if you would like to give it an aged look or simply varnish it with regular indoor varnish. Oiling with a modern furniture oil is also acceptable or a fast finish can be applied using a clear spray lacquer. Spend some time on this step for a more professional looking finish. (See Finishing Suggestions, Appendix A.)

Pins

19. Carefully hammer in the hitch pins leaving just enough pin protruding to wind the string around (13). Screw in the tuning pins (14). Leave a few turns unturned for pulling the string taut later.

Stringing

20. Use number 7 (.018") or number 8 (.020") music wire to string your dulcimer. Large hardware stores or music stores may carry such stock or you may have to research sources and send away for this item. One roll of wire is usually enough to string several dulcimers. An-

other possibility to investigate is that an instrument maker in your town may sell you enough wire to string your dulcimer.

21. String up the top two and bottom two courses first using the method

.12 *Apply veneer (optional step)*

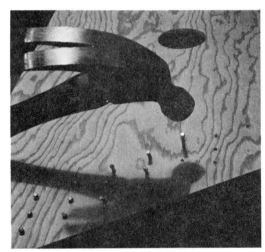

13 *Carefully hammer in hitch pins*

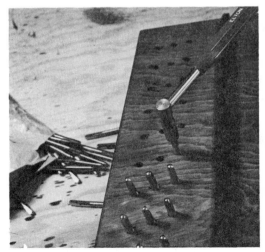

14 *Screw in tuning pins*

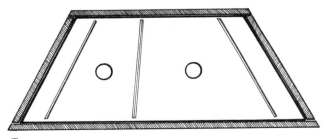

J

shown in the diagram (K) (15). (If you have two gauges of strings use number 7's on the top six courses and number 8's on the bottom half.) This method of stringing eliminates the need to tie a loop in the end of each string (16). Start with tuning pin number 1, loop string around pin twice and run string across to hitch pin number 1, then over to the comparable hitch pin in the next course, loop, and back again to the relative tuning pin. After the strings have been put on top and bottom courses, slip the bridge under the strings, tighten the strings to the prescribed pitches, and adjust the bridge placement until the interval of a perfect fifth is achieved on both high and low courses. A musician can help you if this seems troublesome. String up number 2 and number 3 lengths consecutively. The strings should be wound as close to the base of the tuning pins and hitch pins as possible so that they will "break" over the side bridges securely and not buzz or shift (17). See Tuning Chart (L) below.

22. You will probably have to retune the instrument several times before it finally settles. A quiet room and patience (along with a pitch pipe, piano, etc.) can make this a meditative process rather than a chore.

Mallets

23. The mallets or hammers are about 8" to 10" long and about 1/4" wide. There are an infinite number of hammer styles but the following design is basic to most (M). Use a hardwood. Felt or leather may be glued to the face of each hammer if you wish a softer sound. Many players have several sets of hammers to make different tones and contrasting styles.

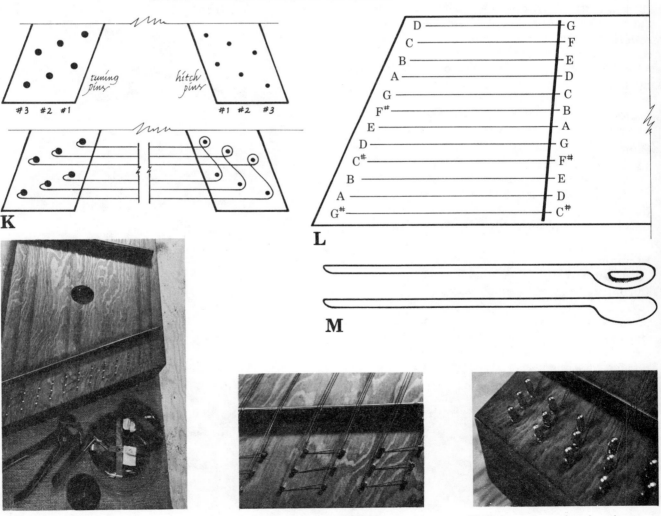

15 *String up the dulcimer.*

16 *String pattern at hitch pins.*

17 *String pattern of tuning pins*

PLAYING SUGGESTIONS

Playing the hammered dulcimer by ear is an interesting way to begin. However, if you know some of the basics of musical technique this will help you to explore the instrument and pick out familiar melodies.

Set the dulcimer on a table and play it from either a standing or sitting level. The instrument is often propped up in back so that it is angled thus making the higher notes closer to the player. Special stands and stools are often made for the dulcimer but these are certainly not a necessity. The most important consideration is to make sure that you are comfortable and can be relaxed while you play.

You will find the three major keys of D, G, C by beginning the scale on the right side of the bridge and switching to the left side halfway up the scale like this:

In addition to these three major scales there are their relative minor scales and other modal scales. You will discover these as you progress. More information and instruction are available from the literature that has been written about the instrument (see Appendix C).

The trick to playing smoothly (especially in fast passages) is to alternate your sticking so that one stick does not play too many consecutive notes or that you do not cross your hands. If you spend some time when you are learning each tune to figure out the sticking you will find that you will not have to unlearn awkward passages later.

A BEGINNER'S SONG

If you read music you can figure out most tunes after some initial orientation. There is, however, a technique of notation known as tablature which may make playing easier. It is simply a system of numbers instead of notes. Many instrument books for beginners use tablature systems to good advantage. There are instruments such as the guitar and banjo that have developed standardized systems; others such as the hammered dulcimer have contrasting systems which depend on the author. I have indicated tablature with numbers for this song. Number 1 string is on the low end or the end closest to you. String numbers on the right side of the bridge will be indicated with parentheses. The tune below is in the key of G so the scale will be notated like this:

This song, "Short'nin' Bread," is in quarter notes (♩) which get one beat each and half notes (♩) which get two beats each. Establish a steady beat and start with the right mallet on number 8 which is the G on the left side of the bridge. Proceed in the following manner:

G	C		D	G		C	F
F#	B		C#	F#		B	E
E	A		B	E		A	D
D	G		A	D		G	C
G Scale			D Scale			C Scale	

(5) (6) (7) (8) 5 6 7 8

8 6 5 6	8 6 5 -	8 6 5 6	(7) (6) (5) -	Repeat
R L R L	R L R	R L R L	R L R	

(5) 6 5 6	(5) 6 5 -	(5) 6 5 6	(7) (6) (5) -	Repeat
R L R L	R L R	R L R L	R L R	

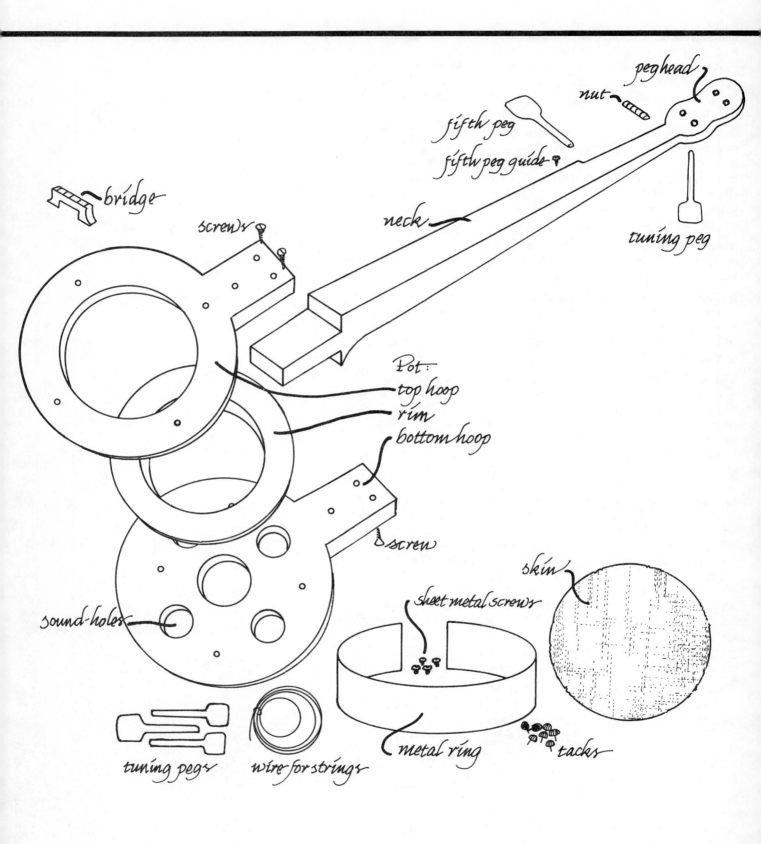

fifth peg

fifth peg guide

nut

peghead

tuning peg

neck

bridge

screws

Pot:
top hoop
rim
bottom hoop

screw

sound-holes

sheet metal screws

skin

metal ring

tacks

tuning pegs

wire for strings

Parts of the Fretless Banjo

Ten centuries ago, Arabian people were playing an instrument called a rebec. This is thought to be the ancient forerunner of the banjo. A rebec is made of an animal skin stretched over a hollow gourd. A crude neck holding three gut strings is attached to the gourd. The instrument was popular and as the Islam culture spread to other areas, the rebec was carried with it. It was Negro slaves who brought the rebec to North America.

In 1785, Thomas Jefferson noted that the "banjar" as it was called, was the most popular instrument of American Negroes. The instrument flourished and by the end of the eighteenth century, four-string tenor and plectrum banjos had been developed. The first five-string fretless banjo was built by Joel Walker Sweeney. Joel Sweeney was raised in Appomattox, Virginia and was a traveling musician. He once played banjo to Queen Victoria at a command performance. His first five-string banjo is now on display at the Los Angeles County Museum in California.

Fretless banjos were built in the Appalachian Mountains by farmers and backwoodsmen who could not afford to buy the fretted, store-bought variety of banjo. The earliest fretless banjos were built of materials obtained from nearby forests. The neck and pot (resonating chamber) were carved and shaped from black walnut or yellow poplar, hickory, maple, cherry, or any other hardwood that was available. Most of the shaping and carving was accomplished with a drawknife, spokeshave, pocket knife, rasp, and file. Then a racoon or squirrel or cat would be caught and skinned. After hair was removed from the hide, the wet hide was then stretched over the banjo pot and was tacked or laced on. As the hide dried, it would tighten. The neck of the banjo was then bolted or screwed on. Tuning pegs were hand carved and roughly fitted into holes in the peghead which had been drilled with an auger or a reamer. Wire or gut strings were added and the fretless banjo was ready to be played.

Much variation in fretless banjo construction occurred throughout the southern Appalachian states. These variations may be classed into four major "pot" styles:
1. Wooden pot with wooden head or top.
2. Wooden pot with hide head stretched over the pot.
3. Wooden pot with wooden flange and hide head stretched over a metal hoop under the flange.
4. Wooden or metal pot with hide or synthetic head stretched over a metal tone ring and held on with a metal flange and brackets (i.e., store-bought variety).

Endless variety exists in the length, width, peg head shape, and method of attachment of the neck. Some banjos have been made from cigar boxes or cake tins. They all play well, for the fretless banjo, unlike the violin and guitar, had no Stradivarius or Martin to dictate what the "perfect sound" should be.

The fretless banjo is usually played by one who has learned to play in the traditional frailing or clawhammer style on a normal fretted banjo (although I prefer the sound and feel of the older style). Playing the fretless banjo requires some patience and practice because your fingers have to "stop" the notes exactly where the frets would be on a fretted banjo. In this way fretless banjo playing is similar to fiddle playing.

82

There are many ways of building a fretless banjo. Perhaps the easiest way is to buy a banjo or banjo kit and remove the frets from the fingerboard. Glue a thin strip of ebony or rosewood over the old fingerboard and then proceed with the assembly. The style of banjo construction described here is based on the Appalachian Mountain model as described in *Foxfire 3*, a book which describes a variety of mountain crafts. Consult Appendix C for other publications relating to the banjo.

MATERIALS

A slab of 1/2" plywood or solid wood 4' long and 1' wide from which the top, back, and hoop will be cut

Hardwood fingerboard block approximately 28" long, 2-1/2" wide, and 2" deep

One tin ring 6" in diameter and 1-1/2" deep

Rawhide calfskin 8" in diameter

Five violin pegs (or whittle your own)

Bridge and nut

ASSEMBLY
Patterns

1. After carefully studying the diagrams on pages 80 and 84 and gathering the necessary materials, transfer the designs for the top, back, and hoop onto the 1/2" solid or plywood stock (A). Solid hard-wood actually makes a better instrument; however, I suggest plywood for a first project because it is cheaper and requires much less preparation than hardwood does. If hardwood is used, you must resaw it to the proper thickness and laminate the pieces edge to edge to achieve the proper width.

Hoop

2. Unless the hoop is cut from 1" stock it is necessary to glue two 1/2" pieces

2 *Remove center of hoop with jigsaw*

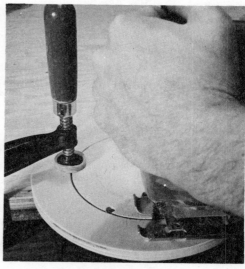

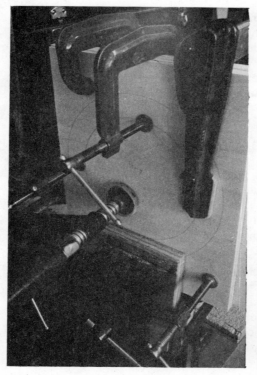

1 *Glue and clamp hoop in a vise*

3 *Remove center of top with jigsaw*

together to achieve the proper thickness (1). After the glue has dried cut a 6-1/2" circle out of the center. Drill a small hole to start the jigsaw blade; then cut slowly and carefully around the circle. Now cut around the outside diameter of the hoop. A band saw may be used for all outside cuts (2).

Top

3. Using the same procedure cut a 6" hole in the middle of the top and then around the outside periphery and the tongue that will overlap the fingerboard (3).

4. Cut out the back. Carefully file and sand the three above components into smooth even shapes (4).

Fingerboard

5. Taking your time, transfer the fingerboard diagram to the fingerboard stock (A). Draw the top view and the side view onto the wood. Double check all lines and measurements. You may wish to make an actual-size pattern of the fingerboard on paper first and then trace it onto the wood. Make sure the fifth peg is on the proper side. Some left-handed players place it on the other side.

Cutting the Fingerboard

6. As you band saw the fingerboard you may find yourself cutting off part of the pattern you will need for a later cut. I usually cut as much of one profile as possible without actually cutting it off. Then I cut the other facets and finally complete the initial cut last. An alternative method is to cut all of one facet and then draw on the other pattern and cut it out. It is important to think through the process carefully before doing any cutting (B).

First Fitting

7. Set up all the pieces and begin rough shaping the parts to fit properly (5) (6). This is simply to check for any discrepencies that might have occurred thus far in the procedure.

4 *Back, hoop, and top of banjo*

5 *Mock-up of banjo before gluing*

6 *Fingerboard/pot junction*

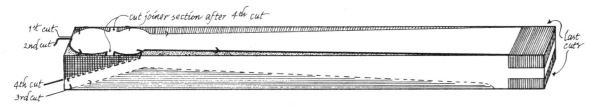

B

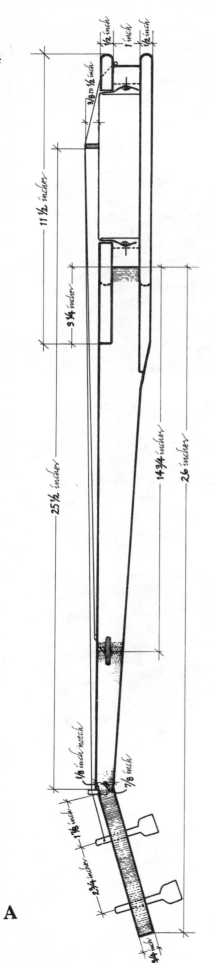

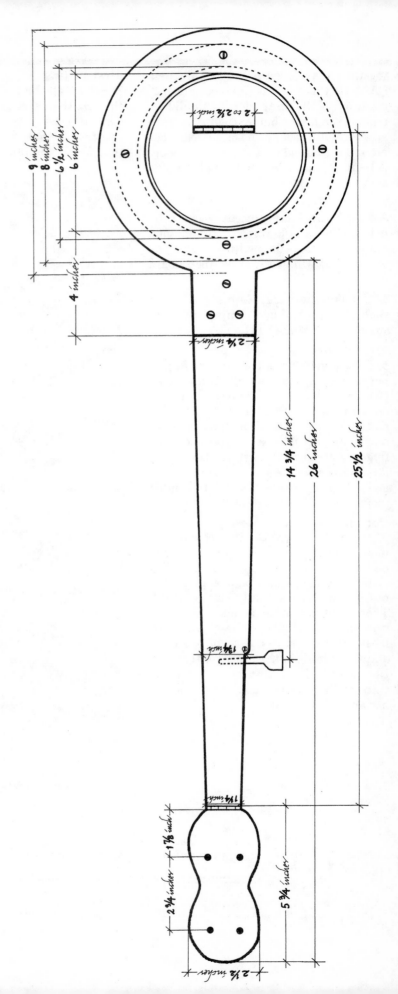

A

Shaping Fingerboard

8. With a rasp, file, spokeshave, and sandpaper shape the back of the fingerboard until it is rounded and smooth (7). Shape the peg head to your liking. Sand the top of the fingerboard perfectly flat and smooth. Study other banjo fingerboards to get the right shape.

Peg Holes

9. Drill holes for pegs with a bit that is slightly smaller than the diameter of your pegs (8). Drill the fifth peg hole (9). Final shaping will be done later.

Make sure the holes are far enough apart so that the peg heads will not collide when turned.

Metal Ring

10. Make the ring which the skin stretches over from any 6" can or metal hoop. I simply cut a piece of sheet metal to fit the diameter of the top hole (actually a little smaller to compensate for the thickness of the skin) and 1-1/2" deep so that the top of the ring will be flush with the top face (A). Small sheet metal screws in predrilled holes seem to be easiest for stabilizing the ring (10)

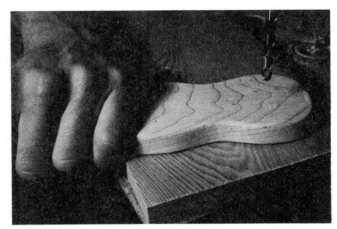

8 *Drill peg holes*

7 *Shape fingerboard with spokeshave*

10 *Metal ring construction*

9 *Fifth peg hole position*

11 *Sheet metal screws placement*

(11); however, spot welding, braizing, or soldering are more satisfactory if equipment is available. The back will eventually hold the ring in tight against the tension of the skin.

Sound-holes and Final Fitting

11. Drill or saw a hole, pattern, or pattern of holes into the back (12) (13). Circles and hearts are the most traditionally used shapes. Sand all edges smooth. Fit all pieces together to make sure they align properly and make a snug fit (14) (15).

Screws

12. Using 1-1/4" screws (brass screws give a good appearance) in predrilled and countersunk holes (there are bits that will drill and countersink at the same time) put the instrument together (16) (17) (18). File and sand the joint where the fingerboard joins the top, back, and hoop (19).

String Holes

13. Drill five small holes at the base of the instrument through the top piece (C). Angle the holes to match the trajectory of the strings as they "break" over the bridge (D).

12 *Circular drill bit makes back sound-holes*

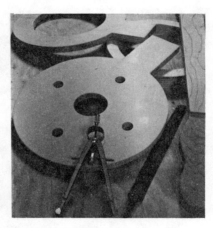

13 *Sound-hole pattern*

14 *Mock-up (be sure to check alignment of fingerboard to hoop)*

15 *Mock-up of banjo pot*

16 *Preparation for drilling*

Finish

14. Disassemble and sand all components with care. Finish by staining if you wish and varnishing, oiling, or lacquering. (See section on finishing, p. 135.)

Skin

15. A thin gauge of calfskin or goatskin (the old-timers would use catskin, usually from their neighbor's cat) is needed for the vibrating membrane. Cut an 8" diameter disc of skin and soak it in water for a few hours (20). (See the section on drumskins, p. 56 for more information.)

18 *Assemble fingerboard to pot*

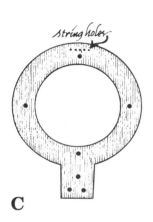

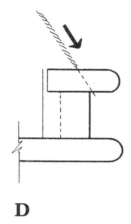

C   D

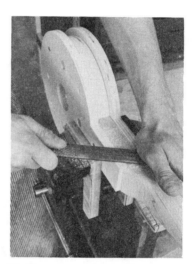

19 *Fit components exactly*

17 *Predrill screw holes*

20 *Preparing skin for banjo pot*

Final Shaping of Peg Holes

16. Meanwhile, with a violin reamer or a rat-tail file, carefully shape each peg hole so that the pegs fit snugly and turn smoothly (21) (22). If you use a rat-tail file, turn the file counterclockwise to remove wood, otherwise it will simply screw itself in and get stuck.

17. Assemble the banjo except for the back (23). Cut a small 3/4" wide strip of sheet metal to help hold the skin in position while you tack it in place with furniture tacks (24). In order to prevent the skin from becoming too tight after it dries, place a small disc or circular object about 3/4" deep under the skin as you tack (25). Since different skins react in different ways, experience must be your final teacher; however, this method should allow the skin to dry to the required tension.

After you have tacked the skin at one inch intervals around the interior of the hoop (25), replace the small hoop with the 1-1/2" sized hoop, trim off excess, and screw on back (26). Put this aside and let it stand for twenty-four hours. Resist the urge to tap it.

5th String Guide

18. Place a small screw with a slot head on the fingerboard to act as a guide for the fifth string (E).

21 *Pegs, reamers, and files*

22 *Shaping peg holes*

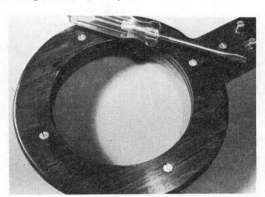

23 *Assembly and preparation for positioning of skin*

24 *Small ¾" width sheet metal ring used to facilitate tacking*

Nut

19. Ebony, bone, or plastic are usually used for the nut. Any hardwood will suffice. Cut it so that it fits the width of the fingerboard. Shape and glue in place (27). With a fine sawblade or knife-file (available at jewelers' outlets) cut four slots into the nut as shown (F). The larger strings will require slightly larger slots. Cut them at a slight angle so that they will slope up from the pegs and pass out of the slot just barely (1/32") above the fingerboard (G).

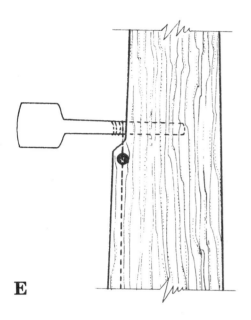

E

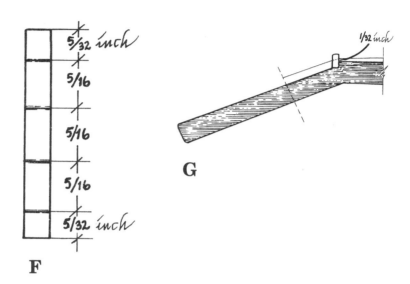

F

G

25 *Tacking procedure*

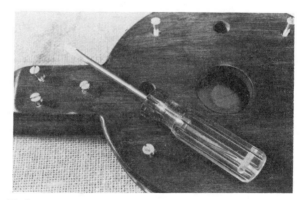

26 *Screw back on pot section*

27 *Position of nut*

Bridge

20. The height and width of the bridge are a matter of personal preference depending on the experiences of the player. Usually however the height of the bridge will be between 3/8" to 1/2" high and about 2" to 2-1/2" long (28) (29). Fine shallow slots on a very slight angle are cut into the bridge with not more than 3/8" between each slot (H). Examine factory-made banjos for bridge designs or simply buy an already made bridge from a music store. It is more in keeping with tradition however to whittle your own. Remember that the large strings will require slightly enlarged slots.

Strings

21. Medium gauge ball-end strings work well and may be found in sets at most music stores. Pass string through the hole at the base of the instrument (30) and clip off excess string leaving 3" to 4" of string to twist around peg (31) (32).

String Length

22. Measure approximately 25-1/2" from nut to bridge.

Tuning

23. Fretless banjos of this sort have numerous tunings. The instrument can be tuned to normal banjo tunings but two or three keys lower. This instrument is not designed to accommodate the great string tension of the modern reinforced banjo.

A suggested tuning:

    5th — E (highest note)
    4th — B (lowest note)
    3rd — E (one octave lower than 5th)
    2nd — G#
    1st — B

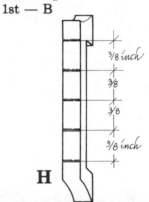

H

28 *Bridge pattern*

29 *Bridge placement*

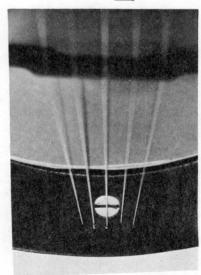

30 *String holes*

Many good books and records describing how to play this popular instrument are readily available. The learning process, however, is quicker and easier if you get an introductory lesson or two from an experienced teacher. If you have previous experience on a stringed instrument you may be able to explore the banjo fruitfully on your own.

The left hand plays the melody and chords. The fingers must be placed fairly accurately since this instrument has no frets. Try figuring out a familiar tune by working it out slowly at first. Most melodies can be played in first position, that is without moving your hand too far up the fingerboard. Changing among the four long strings (the fifth string is never fingered) should accommodate most melodies.

The right-handed styles of playing include strumming, finger picking, and frailing (striking down on the string to produce the melody with the first or second fingers and flicking the fifth string on off beats). Have a banjo picker demonstrate these techniques in slow motion for you. After that all that remains to make you a good player is to practise, practise, practise.

31 *String attachment at head*

32 *String attachment at fifth peg*

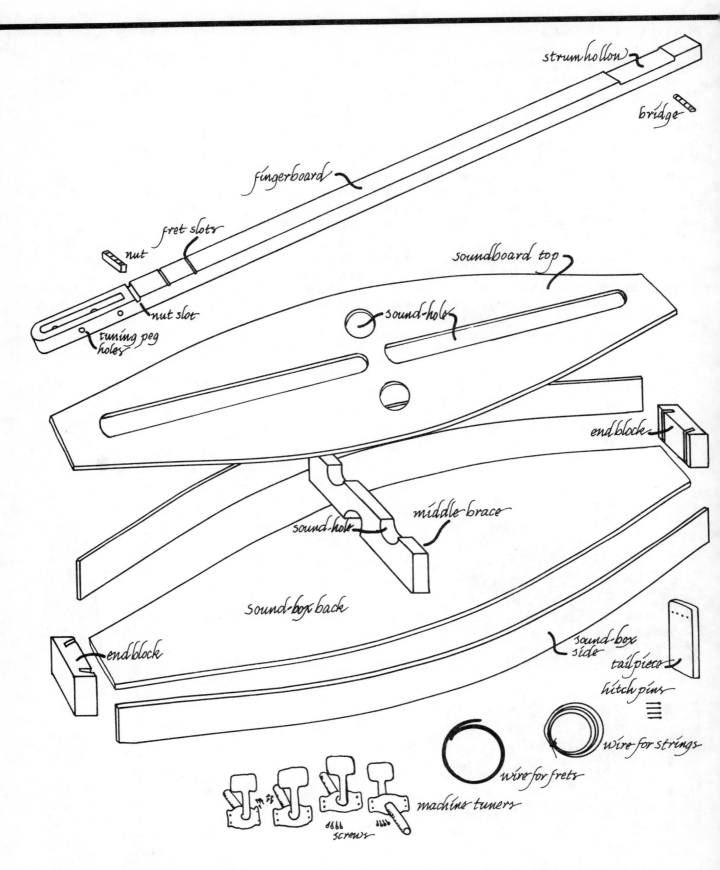

strum hollow

bridge

fingerboard

fret slots

nut

soundboard top

nut slot

sound-hole

tuning peg holes

end block

middle brace

sound-hole

sound-box back

end block

sound-box side

tailpiece

hitch pins

wire for strings

wire for frets

machine tuners

screws

Parts of the Plucked Appalachian Mountain Dulcimer

As is the case with many folk instruments, the origin of the Appalachian Mountain dulcimer is quite uncertain. We do know, however, that its North American manifestation came from European roots where there have been many dulcimer-like instruments. The oldest of these seems to be the German scheitholt documented during the Middle Ages. Other dulcimer-like instruments were known in France (epinette des Vosages), Norway (langesleik), Holland (hummle), Iceland (langspil), and Sweden (humle). One thing that all these instruments had in common was a diatonic fretboard which ran most of the length of the instrument, a fretted string or two on which the melody was noted, and an additional set of drone strings. All the instruments were tuned modally.

When people migrated to the North American continent from Europe, they were unable to carry excess baggage and bulky instruments had to remain behind. But as they settled throughout the eastern seaboard the memory of their homeland music motivated them to build replicas of their old instruments. Since they could not remember exactly how the instrument was made they built their own version of it which became known as the Appalachian Mountain dulcimer and took on its own characteristic construction of three or four strings on a bilaterally symmetrical sound-box often in an "hourglass" or "tear-drop" shape.

Dulcimer (or dulcimore) which means "sweet sound" was a name probably mistakenly borrowed from the older hammered dulcimer also popular in different parts of Europe. The name continued to be used over the years so the Appalachian Mountain variety is now usually prefixed with a "plucked" or "fretted" to differentiate it from its hammered namesake. You can also call it a hog fiddle. The fretted dulcimer may be picked, plucked, feathered, bowed, or struck depending on the tune to be played. Therein lies the charm of a folk instrument. It can be played in any way you wish so long as it pleases the ear. The natural sound quality of the dulcimer is delightful. The happy hours you will spend playing the instrument will certainly compensate for the time you spend with the construction.

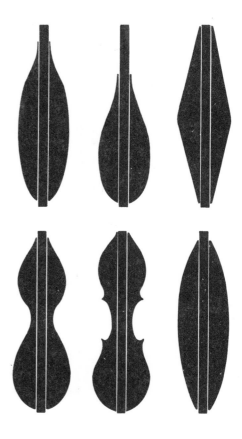

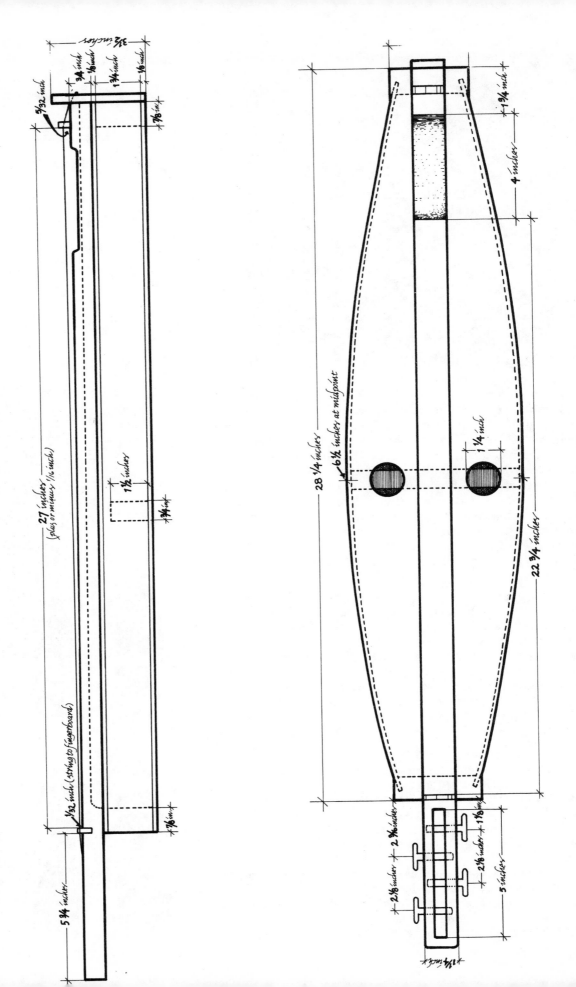

MATERIALS

Piece of 1/8" plywood, approximately 2' x 3'

Stick of hardwood for the fingerboard, 36" x 3/4" x 1-1/4"

2 end blocks, 3" x 1-3/4" x 7/8"

Middle brace of softwood, 6-1/4" x 1-1/2" x 3/4"

Ebony wood, plastic, or bone for nut and bridge

Tuners

Frets

Strings

Note If solid stock woods are desired instead of plywood for the body, follow the resawing instructions on p. 65. Use 1/8" hardwoods for back and sides and 3/32" to 1/8" softwood for the soundboard. You may have to glue these plates edge to edge to achieve the desired width. A book on guitar construction will provide you with the details for gluing and clamping.

ASSEMBLY
Initial Cuts

1. From the piece of 1/8" plywood cut two rectangles (which will become the top and back) measuring 29" x 6-1/2" and a pair of sides measuring 29" x 1-3/4". If the plywood has a tendency to warp or twist do not worry for this will come right in the end. Simply be a little more conscientious when weighting and clamping the glued parts to make sure that an even bond is achieved. Next, cut two end blocks from your hardwood piece. It is important that the end blocks be the exact height of the side pieces. End blocks measure 3" x 1-3/4" x 7/8" (A). The middle brace may be cut from any type of wood including plywood as long as it measures 6-1/4" long, 1-1/2" high, and 3/4" to 1" wide.

End Block Slots

2. Slots must now be cut into each end block so that the sides fit snugly into them (B). This can be done carefully with a hand saw or band saw (1). The more precise the fit of the sides the better (2).

1 *Cut slots in end blocks*

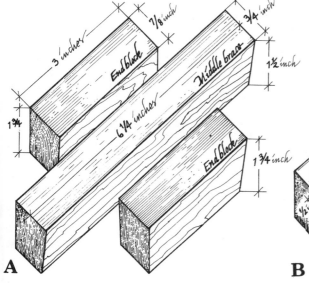

A

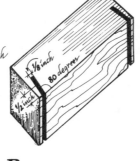

B

2 *Put sides in place*

Middle Brace

3. After cutting the middle brace (6-1/4" x 1-1/2" x 3/4"), cut scallops into it to allow sound and vibration to pass freely through it (3).

Mock-up and Pattern

4. Assemble sides, end blocks, and brace without glue (4). Place this assemblage onto the 1/8" plywood piece that you have chosen for the back, centering the end blocks on each end (5). Hold down assemblage firmly and draw a pencil line around the outside periphery of the sides onto the back (6). This determines the shape of your dulcimer.

Cut Top and Back

5. Tape the top and back pieces together so that the penciled pattern is visible. Cut about 1/16" outside the penciled line with a coping saw, band saw, or jigsaw (7). *Do not cut inside the line.*

Glue End Blocks and Brace

6. Again mock up the sides with end blocks and middle brace in place on the back piece. Clamp or weight this assemblage and check along all joints making sure everything fits properly (8). Mark the position of the end blocks and middle brace on the back to guide you while you glue and clamp. End blocks and brace may be glued one at a time or simultaneously depending on your method of clamping (9) (10). With a very thin stick, clear glue out of the slots in the end blocks (11). If you neglect to do this the sides will not fit into the slots properly and the glue will be difficult to remove after it has dried.

3 *Middle brace scallops placement*

4 *Side, end block, and brace assembly*

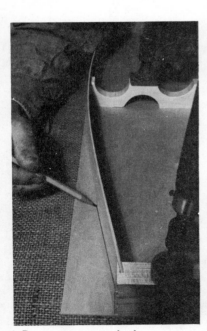

6 *Draw pattern onto back*

7 *Saw top and back simultaneously (note stock taped together)*

5 *Mock-up on sound-box back stock*

8 *Check for accurate fit*

Sides Glued

7. After the glue on the end blocks and brace have dried, place side pieces into position and make sure they are the same height as the end blocks by checking at the top of each slot. File or plane if necessary. An easy method of gluing the sides in place is to put the sound-box on a flat surface and place a flat board over the whole sound-box area. Find heavy cinderblocks, bricks, stones, or metal weights that will apply even pressure. Try this without glue first to ensure a good fit.

Finally, apply an ample bead of glue along the bottom edge of each side, in every slot (spread with small stick), and on each end of the middle brace. Put sides into place, put board on top, and weight. Double check for a good glue joint between sides and back. If some spot appears not to touch properly try shifting the weight or slip small shims under the back to force the gap to close.

Fingerboard

8. The fingerboard (34" x 3/4" x 1-1/4") must now be marked according to diagram (C). Using the band saw and a file or two, cut out the strum hollow about 1/8" deep (12). Smooth with sandpaper. The sound of the final instrument can be improved appreciably by hollow-

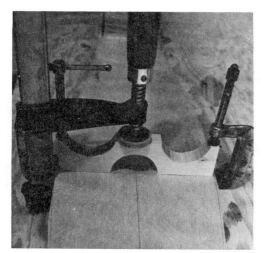
9 *Glue middle brace into position*

10 *Glue end blocks in place*

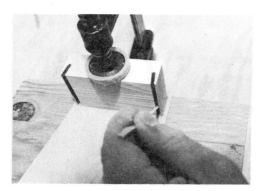
11 *Remove excess glue from slots*

12 *Hollow out strum hollow*

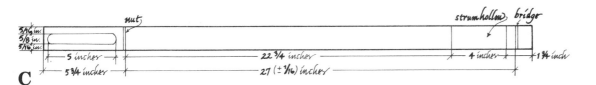
C

ing out the fingerboard. Although this step is not entirely necessary it can be done with a table saw (13) or a router (14). However, care must be taken because this is not an easy cut to make. The hollowed trough which is 3/4" wide and 1/2" deep will stop 6" short from the end which is to be the peg box (15). This may be done by starting cuts from the end with the strum hollow and lifting wood or stopping the saw at a visible pencil mark on the fingerboard.

Peg Head

9. Draw the peg slot onto the fingerboard according to the diagram. The slot can be made by either drilling out the ends with a 5/8" bit and completing it with a jigsaw (16) (17) or by drilling out the entire slot area and finishing by filing it uniform. Sand the entire fingerboard smooth. The fingerboard *must* be perfectly flat.

Nut

10. The string length (distance between the nut and the bridge) is approximately 27". Measure and mark the position of the nut and bridge. The nut should be just in front of the peg slot and the bridge is just beyond the strum hollow. Cut a slot across the fingerboard with a saw to hold the nut. You may make the nut from bone, ebony, hard plastic, or any very hard wood. It should measure about 1-1/4" x 1/8" x 1/4" and fit snugly into the slot. Do not glue it in yet. Bridge measurements are the same as for the nut.

Scale and Fret Slots

11. Using a small square take the measurement from the nut and mark off the following fret positions (D). Mark as accurately as possible. Now comes the hurdle of finding 3' to 4' of fretwire and a saw to match. I have found that banjo

13 *Hollow out fingerboard with table saw*

14 *Use router to hollow out fingerboard*

15 *Trough stops six inches from end of peg head*

16 *Drill peg head slots*

17 *Cut out peg head slots*

fretwire works best for dulcimers but guitar wire is sufficient. Call the music repair shops in your town and speak with the maker or repairman about buying a length of wire (sometimes it is already cut into 1-1/2" to 2" pieces) and about an appropriate saw that will match the fretwire. Fine and extra fine coping saw blades will usually cut a slot that will hold the fret snug. Some makers buy a fine-toothed dovetail saw and carefully grind down the set of the teeth on a whet stone to just the right degree. Experiments and patience are in order to find a working combination.

Fretting

12. Practise on a scrap piece of wood first, then cut a shallow slot with the saw just deep enough to receive the tine of the fret (18). Cut the fret to length (1-1/4") (19) and carefully but firmly tap it into the slot. To keep from damaging the fret it may help to just get it started into the slot, place a piece of wood on the fret, and hammer the wood to set the fret firmly into the slot (20). If it gets bent in the process or the slot is too big to hold it well, remove the fret, straighten it or cut a new one, and glue it neatly into place with white glue or epoxy glue. It is usually advisable to cut the frets a little longer than the width of the fingerboard and clip or file off the excess after they are all in place.

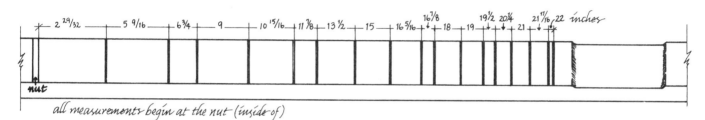

all measurements begin at the nut (inside of)

D

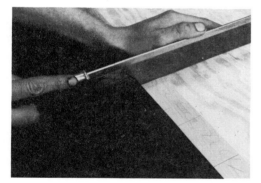

18 *Cut fret slots*

19 *Cut frets to length for slots*

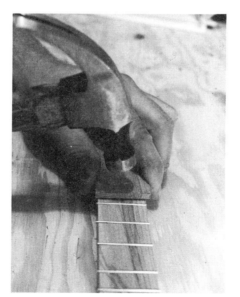

20 *Use block of wood to set frets into fingerboard*

Dressing the Frets

13. With a straight rule check to see that all the frets are level with one another and of a uniform height. If not, carefully lay a large file (or fine sandpaper glued to a long flat stick) on the frets and gently work them level. File the ends of the frets until they are perfectly flush with the side of the fingerboard.

Carefully, round the ends of the frets using a fine metal file (21) or fine sandpaper and then polish them with steel wool (22). Study existing fretted instruments to get the right shape. Run your fingers along the edges to check for edges that might nick fingers.

Peg Holes

14. Drill holes into the peg head (23) to match the tuners you have found. You may choose to have three strings or four strings. A three-string dulcimer is more traditional and a little easier to play. A four-string dulcimer has a bit more tone. Do not place the tuners permanently at this stage.

Top

15. Place the fingerboard directly down the center of the top piece or soundboard and make small marks at each end to help position it later when gluing. If you have hollowed out the fingerboard it will further enhance the tone of the instrument to cut a long slot in the soundboard to match the fingerboard thus allowing the vibrations easier access into the sound-box. Using a long rule mark the slot on the soundboard so that it will match the exact width of the fingerboard slot. I have left a little bridge of wood in the center for extra stability. Next, cut the slot by drilling holes at either end and using a coping saw with a coarse blade to remove the wood (24). Clamp your work down securely to ease cutting. A jigsaw will also do a good job. Many makers cut the top into two separate pieces and glue it to the fingerboard.

After cutting the slot, finish the edges with a file and sandpaper.

Sound-holes

16. The easiest form for the sound-hole is a circle. These can be drilled into the top. In this example the sound-holes were drilled with a 1-1/4'' spade bit (25). When using a large bit, be sure to clamp

21 *File ends of frets*

22 *Placed and polished frets*

23 *Peg hole position*

the work down firmly. Arrangements of circles of different sizes and fancy sound-holes are options. Heart shapes are traditional (see Appendix A). The size or placement of sound-holes does not seem to be bound by any predetermined rules for simple folk instruments; however, the importance of this factor increases in direct relationship to the sophistication of the instrument. In the violin, for instance, the number and placement of sound-holes are of utmost importance.

Fingerboard to Top

17. Position the fingerboard again on the soundboard and check to make sure that the slots match and the peg head is extended beyond one end. Practise placing the fingerboard and place a flat board on top to weight for pressure. Use clamps if they are available. Apply glue down each rail of the fingerboard, place it onto the soundboard very carefully, and hold it tightly for a couple of minutes. Do not let it slide out of line. Then place board and weight in place (26). Let dry.

Top to Bottom

18. Buy a box or two of heavy rubber bands for the next step unless you have plenty of clamps. You may want to make your own violin-style clamps. Fit the top assemblage onto the sound-box and check for good contact all around the instrument. High spots can be carefully planed or filed. With a friend to help, try putting a few rubber bands around the instrument so that they apply the most pressure around the lip of the soundboard where it joins the sides. Once you are satisfied in this respect, apply a good bead of glue all around the top edge of the sound-box (the edges of the sides and the end blocks). Carefully position the top onto the sound-box and hold tightly for a couple of minutes. Your friend can hold onto it while you put on the rubber bands (27). Clamp or weight any spots that need extra pressure. Let dry.

24 *Remove wood from sound-box top below fingerboard*

25 *Drill out sound-holes*

26 *Glue fingerboard to top*

27 *Glue top to bottom part of dulcimer*

Trim

19. Begin the finishing stages by filing or planing the edges of the instrument (a spokeshave works well) (28). This may take some time. Be careful not to chip the edge of the plywood. Sand all the edges slightly round to give the instrument a nice look and feel. Even up any overhanging parts. Reglue and clamp any parts that did not join properly the first time. Round all edges and corners on the peg head.

Tailpiece

20. Because I used the table saw in this example to hollow out the fingerboard thus leaving the end of the board open, a tailpiece may be desirable. If a router had been used and the fingerboard was left closed on the end, hitch pins (1/2" finishing nails) could simply be ham-mered into the end of the fingerboard (29). For the tailpiece cut a small block of wood the width of the fingerboard and drill three small holes to receive the string ends. Glue and screw tailpiece onto end block (30) (31) (32). Let dry.

Sanding

21. Beginning with a number 120 grit sandpaper, sand out all scratches, rough spots, and glue smears. A sharp chisel may be needed to remove dried glue from corners and crevases. Sand the entire instrument finally with number 220 grit sandpaper. Time spent here will be rewarded with a better appearance of the finished instrument.

Finishing

22. See Finishing Suggestions in Appendix A.

28 *Plane edges smooth*

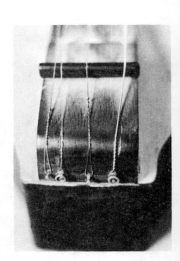

29 *Example of hitch pin and string attachment*

30 *Tailpiece assembly*

31 *Drill string holes in tailpiece*

Tuners

23. Put tuners onto the peg head and mark the holes where the screws will be. Predrill the screw holes with a small bit just slightly smaller than the screws. Some tuners (like inexpensive banjo tuners) require no screws. Fasten these as instructed by the manufacturer (33).

Nut and Bridge

24. Mark nut and bridge as shown in diagram (E) (depending on whether you are using three or four strings). With a very fine saw or knife-file cut slots at a slight angle on the nut to within 1/32" above the surface of the fretboard (if you have used banjo fretwire). The bridge should be cut from the same material as the nut and slots cut to within 3/16", again angled, from the surface of the fretboard. If guitar fretwire has been used the tolerances will be a little higher.

The next process is called setting the action of the instrument. In essence, to set the nut slots, the strings should pass as close to the first fret as possible without buzzing. To set the slots on the bridge, the strings must pass as close as possible to the third fret when the finger depresses it at the second fret.

When buzzes or rattles occur some troubleshooting and patience may be necessary to eliminate them. Trace them down, figure out the cause, and take a common sense approach to getting rid of them.

Strings

25. Use banjo or guitar strings (34) (35). Ball-end strings should be used if a tailpiece with holes is used. Loop-end strings work well on pitch pins. Use these string gauges: Bass string — .020 or .022; Middle string — .012; Melody string — .010 or .012.

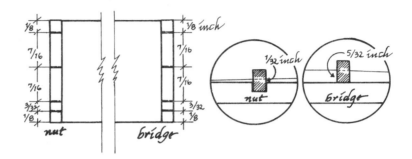

E

33 *Attach tuners to peg head*

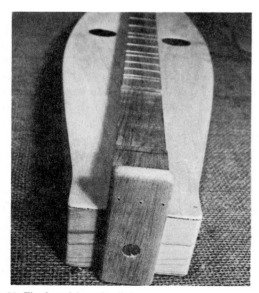

32 *Final position of tailpiece*

34 *String assembly at tailpiece*

35 *Strings at peg head*

TUNING THE APPALACHIAN DULCIMER

Find a quiet place and a comfortable chair with no arms. Put the dulcimer across your lap at a slight angle with the tuning pegs out to your left and the tailpiece next to your right hip. (**Note** If you play left-handed, the strings should be reversed and the dulcimer positioned with the pegs out to your right.) When playing by yourself with no other instruments, tune the instrument to a pitch where it sounds best. Do this by tightening the bass string (the fat string farthest away from you) so that it has good resonance. This is usually a little on the tight side. Never turn the tuning peg without simultaneously plucking the string so that you can hear how fast the tension is increasing.

After you are satisfied with the sound and feel, put a finger behind or to the left of the fourth fret (assuming you're right-handed) on the bass string. One by one tune all the other strings to this pitch. This may take a little juggling and adjusting but do whatever is necessary to accommodate the fingering, plucking and peg turning all at once. This will give you the Ionian mode.

The Ionian mode is the same as the modern major scale. A great number of the songs you will learn use this tuning. The beginning of the scale or "do" is on the melody string (string closest to you) just behind or to the left of the third fret. Try starting at this point. Now, keeping your finger just behind each fret, play up and down the scale only on the melody string while doing a simple strum across all the strings. A large thin pick is usually best for dulcimer strumming.

A Song for Beginners

It is fun to explore the instrument by making up melodies or playing ad libitum until you stumble upon a familiar tune. You may also wish to learn a folk song from scratch. "Aunt Rody" (see Song Selection, p. 141) has become a standard tune for beginning folk instrumentalists. It is authentic, has an easy rhythm, and covers a reasonable range. Establish a medium beat in your head or by tapping your foot. The song has a four-beat pattern per measure, the half notes (d) getting two beats each and the quarter notes ($\flat$) getting one beat each. The song begins on the fifth fret for two beats and progresses at the same pace throughout. Use a single strum per note. It is a pleasant effect to begin the song with the instrument alone, then sing the verses with an occasional solo instrument break. If you are having trouble orienting to all or any of this I would suggest getting an introductory lesson from a teacher or some help from a musician friend. Instructional books or records also help. (See Appendix B for list of suitable books.)

There have been many volumes written about the violin family: its history, its makers, and its every detail have been examined and experimented with throughout the ages. The violin reached its highest level of perfection in the sixteenth, seventeenth, and eighteenth centuries in Cremona, Italy. Stradivarius, Amati, and Guarneri are accepted as the all-time master craftsmen of the violin who brought it to a standard of perfection which is still emulated and copied.

Throughout history experiments have been made to vary the shape, size, and materials of the violin. Indeed, if we examine the "violin-type" instruments of other cultures i.e., bowed stringed instruments, we find an infinite variety of styles, each dependent on the materials found in the environment and the requirements of the music of the area. Bamboo, gourds, animal parts, exotic trees, and even human bones have been utilized for many types of stringed instruments.

Although the shape of the violin seems to have evolved to an accepted standard, that shape is by no means sacred. Savart during the seventeenth century experimented with a trapezoidal violin with good success. An examination of North American folk culture discloses the clever and pragmatic approaches of the "grass roots" craftsmen and musicians towards violin/fiddle construction. Most of us have heard of the cigar-box fiddle, the spike fiddle, or the beggar's fiddle. Although these instruments are certainly not capable of the dynamic quality of the classical violin they nevertheless can produce tones of considerable delicacy and variation, depending of course on the player.

The fiddle I have designed may be classed somewhere between the models of the classical purists and the aboriginal craftsmen. The design is simple but is based on the measurements of a classical violin. It would be easy, therefore, to switch from playing this fiddle to a more sophisticated violin. Orchestral musicians who have played this instrument have commented favorably on its tonal color and playability although most of them, because of their training, require a chin rest to achieve full maneuverability. A chin rest will fit this model; however, I found that some widening at the tailpiece end of the instrument is necessary before it will perfectly accommodate a "store-bought" chin rest. Since most fiddlers play in first position (left hand in one position at nut end of fingerboard not shifting up the fingerboard) and sometimes cradle the fiddle into the elbow area of the arm, the chin rest is not a necessity.

To make an instrument that exactly suits your needs you might like to experiment and incorporate your own ideas. Often, reading other books about violins and the bowed instruments found in other cultures will suggest new methods and details. The insructions here are by no means definitive. Rather, my descriptions will provide the basic measurements and procedure from which you may begin further explorations.

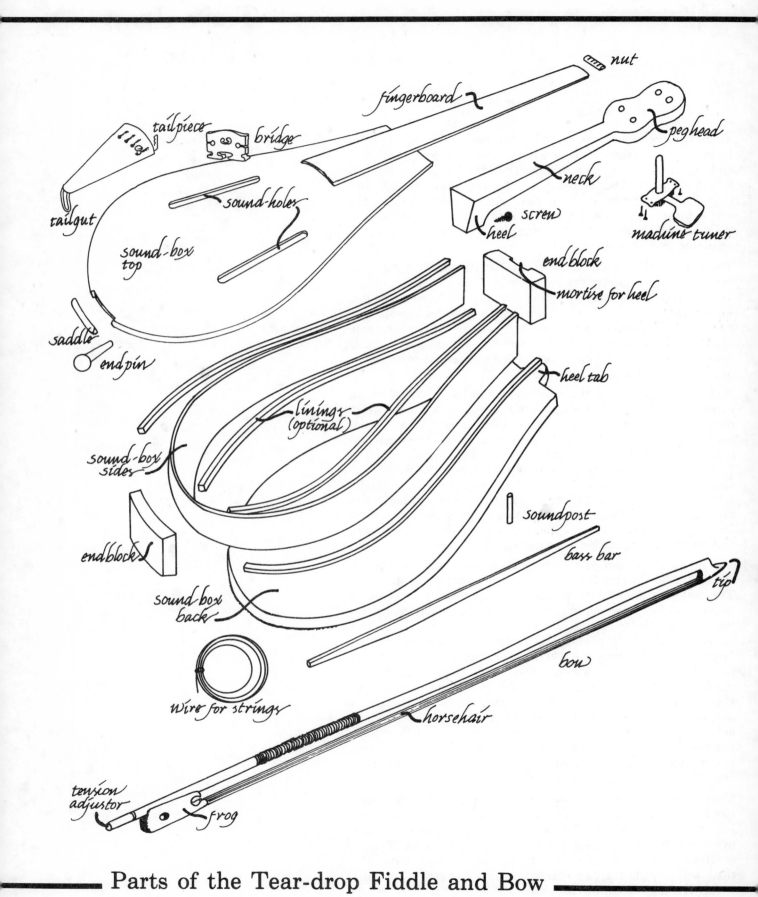

nut

fingerboard

tailpiece

bridge

peghead

neck

tailgut

sound-holes

screw

heel

machine tuner

sound-box top

end block

mortise for heel

saddle

heel tab

endpin

linings (optional)

sound-box sides

soundpost

bass bar

endblock

tip

sound box back

bow

wire for strings

horsehair

tension adjustor

frog

Parts of the Tear-drop Fiddle and Bow

MATERIALS

1/8" plywood (with two good sides) for top and sides

Note Solid stock material may be substituted if you follow the aforementioned parameters (p. 66).

3/8" plywood for the back

Maple block for neck and peg head (10" x 2" x 2")

One violin fingerboard

One violin tailpiece and end pin

A violin bridge

One soundpost (softwood 1/4" dowel)

A strip of softwood for the base bar

Two small maple blocks for the end blocks

One inexpensive violin bow

ASSEMBLY
Sides and End Blocks

1. The idea of using 1/8" plywood which is flexible and bends easily is to bypass the need of jigs and molds which have traditionally been necessary for side formation. Cut a strip of 1/8" plywood 1-3/8" wide and 32" long from stock that has no flaws to insure an even bend. Cut a neck end block 1-3/8" high, 2-1/2" wide, and 5/8" thick from a piece of maple. File or band saw a slight angle on each end of the block so that when the plywood is bent around it is no wider than 5-1/2" at the midpoint (A). Heat and moisture might be used to help the plywood bend into the proper configuration.

Note The 5-1/2" limit ensures that the outside edges will not interfere with the bow when playing the outside strings. This is the reason that classical violins have such a pronounced "waist" at this point.

More pronounced variations in the basic shape may be made with the use of a bending iron or heated pipe over which the wood is carefully pressed and formed. This step must be done if you are using solid wood.

2. After a satisfactory shape is achieved, glue and clamp the end block in place as shown in the photograph (1). This method will hold it straight and prevent it from slipping out of position. Let dry.

3. The tailpiece end block should fit the curve formed by the plywood. From a piece of maple cut a 1-3/8" high, 1-3/4" long, and 5/8" wide piece and sand and file so that this fit is accomplished and glue it so that it is centered perfectly in the curve (2). Let dry.

1 *Glue and clamp sides to end block*

2 *Glue and clamp tailpiece end block*

5½ inches
midpoint
(bowing area)

A

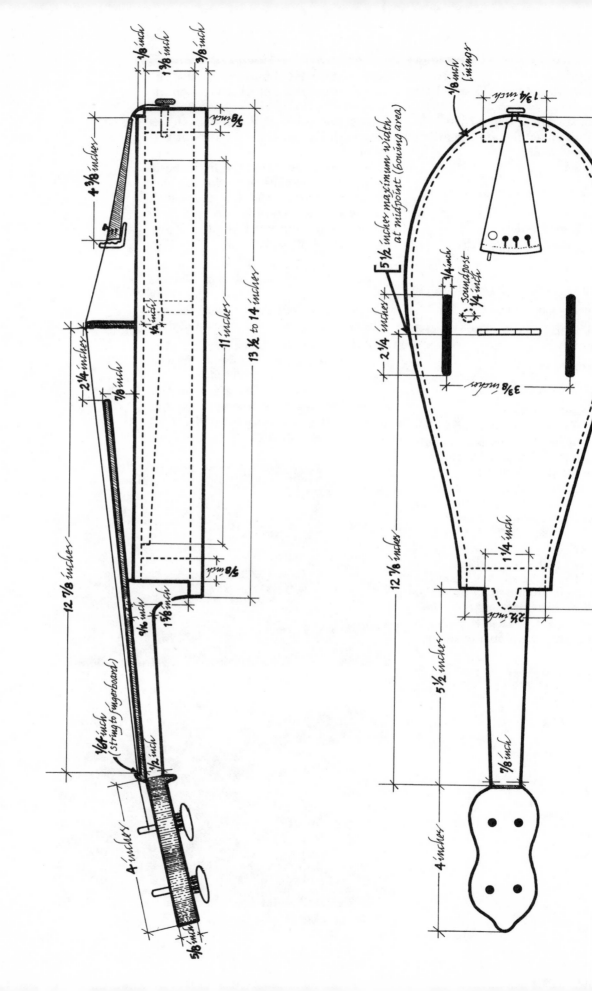

Linings (optional)

4. Cut two thin strips the length of the sides to act as linings. These are to be glued around the inside edges to increase the gluing surface thus increasing the strength of the bond (3). If the linings will not conform exactly to the inside contour use heat and moisture to help make the wood yield. Then, with the use of clothespins, glue the linings in place (4). They should protrude slightly above the sides. Let dry.

5. Either with a sanding board or with a file or plane smooth the top and bottom edges to be sure they are flat and uniform all around.

Back and Top

6. Place the sides and end blocks onto the piece of 3/8" plywood that you have chosen for the back and pencil on its outline.

Note Make sure to leave a little extra tongue at the top of the pattern onto which you will glue the heel of the neck. Next, band saw or coping saw around the pattern, leaving a little extra margin around the edges (5). The top may be cut out in the same fashion from a piece of 1/8" plywood.

Neck and Peg Head

7. Turn your attention now to the neck and peg head. Draw the pattern shown in diagrams (B) (C) (D) onto the top and side of a 10" x 2" x 2" block of maple (6) (7).

Using a band saw carefully cut out the basic form (8). You might refer back to the cutting procedure of the fretless banjo fingerboard. The neck can be rounded

4 *Glue linings to sides; hold with clamps*

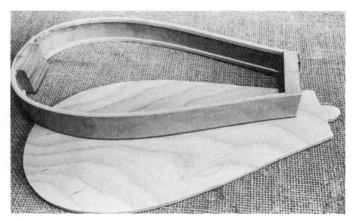

5 *Cut back pattern*

3 *Linings for sound-box*

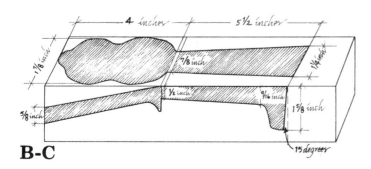

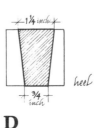

B-C

D

with either a curved spokeshave or a rasp-file combination. It would be most beneficial at this point if you can find a violin to study and use as a model. Otherwise, since this is a relatively simple form of fiddle, use your own judgment for the shaping of the neck and peg head. Carve the heel as shown (9).

8. When the major cut-marks and scratches have been removed by file, sandpaper to smoothness (10).

Sides to Back

9. Using C-clamps, violin clamps, or rubber bands for clamping, glue the sides to the back (11).

6 *Draw neck and peg head pattern (side view)*

7 *Draw neck and peg head pattern (top view)*

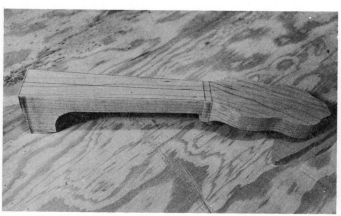
8 *Rough shape of neck and peg head*

9 *Carve the heel*

10 *Round the neck*

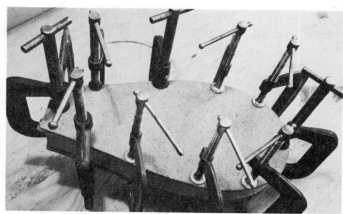
11 *Glue and clamp sides to back*

Note To keep the clamps from denting the wood when pressure is applied, cut an overall clamp pad from a scrap piece of plywood or masonite (12).

Mortising Neck to Sound-box

10. Measure by eye and check carefully with a long ruler to make sure that when the neck is butted to the center of the end block they line up perfectly with the center line (E).

The neck should be at a 15⁰ incline relative to the end block (F).

Pencil the outline of the heel onto the end block and with a knife cut lines just inside your pencil marks along the outline. A sharp chisel and mallet may then be employed to remove the necessary wood so that the heel of the neck fits perfectly into the 1/4'' deep mortise/notch (13).

Fingerboard

11. I have suggested buying an inexpensive fingerboard, tailpiece, and bridge because these are fairly difficult items for the beginning maker to carve. Satisfactory fingerboards may be found in almost any music shop that makes violin repairs or you can send for one from any of the companies listed in Appendix C of this book. Sometimes a white wood dyed black to look like ebony wood (from which most fingerboards are made) can be purchased for a reasonable sum of money.

12 *Use masonite boards as pads to prevent crushing sides and back*

13 *Chisel mortise into end block*

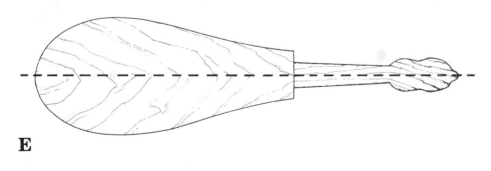

E

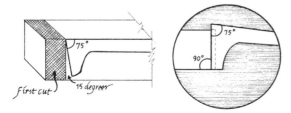

F

112

Mock-up

12. Fit the heel to the end block as shown (14) (15). Do not glue yet. Using a padded clamp, clamp the fingerboard to the neck so that the nut is at the prescribed point. Making sure that the top is lying flat on the sound-box, measure the distance from the top surface of the end of the fingerboard to the top surface of the sound-box. It should be within 1/16" either side of 7/8" (G). If your measurements are not true, make adjustments in the heel of the neck and/or in the angle of the mortise joint. Be sure the base of the heel fits well to the back tab. There are no shortcuts to fitting these crucial elements. Time and careful handwork will eventually do the job. They should fit well since there is considerable tension on this joint.

Top

13. While the top is in position mark the placement of the bridge onto it by measuring from the end of the fingerboard (16). This will determine the placement of the sound-holes which are to be cut next. The bridge is placed at the very midpoint of the sound-holes. From fingerboard to bridge is 2-1/4".

Sound-holes

14. Draw the sound-holes on the top as specified by diagram (H).

Drill the ends of the sound-holes and complete the cut with a coping saw or fret saw (17). File and sand to uniform smoothness.

14 *Fit neck to end block*

15 *Position of heel in end block mortise*

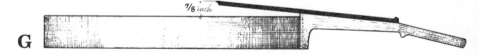
G

16 *Measure placement of bridge*

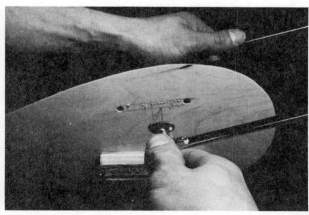
17 *Cut sound-holes*

Bass Bar

15. The bass bar is designed to give strength to the violin top and to help reinforce and transmit the frequencies of the low strings. Cut this bar from a strip of spruce to the dimensions specified (I). The bass bar is to be glued directly under the left foot of the bridge as you look at it from the outside i.e., under the low-string side. It angles in slightly in relationship to the center line moving from bottom to top (18). Glue the bass bar in place with gentle but firm pressure (19).

Top to Sound-box

16. Using the same procedure as you did to cut out and put on the back, glue the top carefully in place (20) (21). Let dry. File and sand all edges flush.

19 *Glue and clamp bass bar*

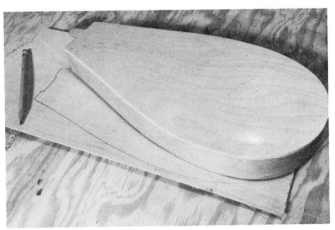

20 *Mark and cut out sound-box top pattern*

21 *Glue and clamp top to sound-box (note use clamping pads to protect top and bottom)*

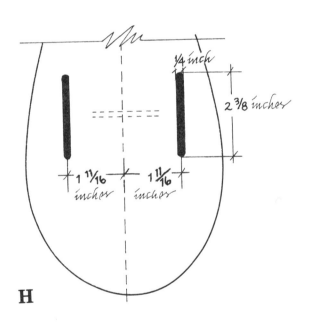

H

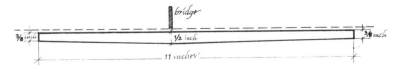

I

18 *Position of bass bar to center line*

17. File the notch of the mortise joint into the top piece and test the fit of the neck and the distance of the end of the fingerboard to the top plate (22).

Neck to Sound-box

18. After you are satisfied with this conjunction, glue the neck to the sound-box and double check its alignment to the center line and the distance of the end of the fingerboard to the top plate. Let dry.

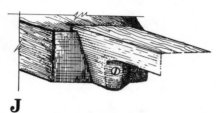

J

For extra reinforcement predrill and countersink a screw through the heel of the neck into the end block (J). Nails and screws are found on some very fine violins for extra stability.

Saddle

19. Chisel a small notch at the end of the tailpiece in which will fit a small piece of ebony or hardwood to prevent the tailpiece/end pin connector from cutting into the edge of the top (23).

End Pin

20. Drill a hole into the tailpiece end block and gradually enlarge it with a round tapered file or a peg-hole reamer so that the end pin fits tightly (24) (25). Glue in place.

22 *Fit neck and fingerboard to sound-box*

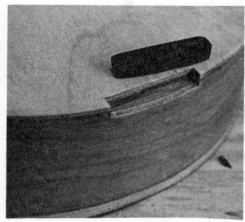

23 *Notch for saddle*

24 *End pin position*

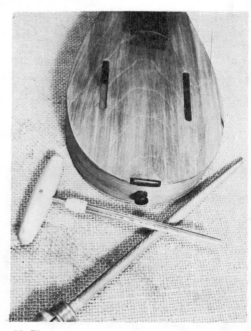

25 *Placement of end pin to sound-box*

Stain

21. If you wish to stain the instrument it will be easiest to do it at this time. Once the fingerboard is glued on it will be more difficult to work under it. However, make sure the fingerboard fits onto the neck well prior to staining.

Fingerboard and Nut

22. Glue the fingerboard and nut into place. Grooves cut into the nut should be 7/32" apart and deep enough so that the distance between the bottom of the string to the fingerboard is 1/64" (K).

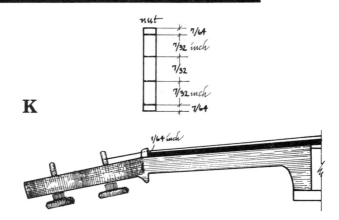

Soundpost

23. The soundpost is made from a length of 1/4" straight-grained spruce. It is lightly wedged between the top and the back of the fiddle to enhance the treble response by setting the back into vibration and to support the top under the great pressure of the strings when they are at full tension. The approximate length of the soundpost can be judged by inserting it into the instrument through the sound-hole and marking the length required. With the help of a soundpost setter or a piece of sharpened heavy wire (coathanger) bent to facilitate setting the post upright once it is inserted into the instrument, position the post 1/8" below the right foot of the bridge (26) Careful assembly of this part may take considerable time. Several adjustments may be needed to make everything fit properly. Final adjustment of the soundpost is done after the strings have been put on.

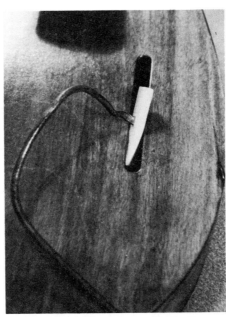

26 *Soundpost and coathanger "setter"*

Tuners

24. Put tuners in place and mark the screw holes with an awl (27). Select a drill bit that is slightly smaller than the screws provided with your tuners and predrill the holes. Carefully screw on the tuners (28) using the proper sized screwdriver.

27 *Mark tuner placement*

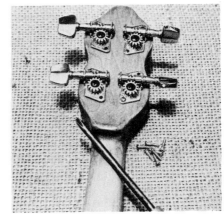

28 *Screws on tuners*

Tail Gut

25. Adjust the tail gut so that the end of the tailpiece is as close as possible to the bottom edge of the instrument (29).

String

26. Wrap the ends of each string around their respective tuning pegs and insert the other end into the tailpiece (30). Take up the slack and set the bridge into position (31). Fine tuners on the tailpiece are not really necessary with machine-head tuners on the peg head but they may help you with fine tuning if this is what you require.

TUNING THE FIDDLE

The second string from the highest is tuned to "concert pitch" which is an A. A tuning fork which has been machined to yield an A of exactly 440 vibrations per second is often used as a standard pitch in orchestras. The third string or next lowest is then tuned to a D. The lowest string is a G and the highest string is tuned to an E. On the first tuning or when changing strings, another round of tuning is necessary because the instrument settles under tension. Final soundpost adjustment is done at this time until the best sound is achieved.

PLAYING SUGGESTIONS

Recently, many instruction books describing a variety of playing styles for the fiddle have been published. There are many excellent books for beginners (see Appendix C of this book).

29 *Tail gut position*

30 *Strings at tuners*

31 *Tailpiece, bridge, strings in final position*

The earliest forms of the harp reach far back into antiquity two to three thousand years B.C. Sumerian and Egyptian harps were either in the form of two pieces forming an angle between which the strings were stretched or an arch which consisted of a curved branch with a sound-box at one end and strings across the gap. The other popular instrument was the lyre which is often referred to in accounts about Greek culture. The harp, however, was certainly the most important instrument in most early cultures and was unrivaled for thousands of years as the first among all known instruments.

Pictoral reliefs carved in stone during the eighth and ninth centuries give the first clue that the harp traveled into Europe and as far as Ireland. In fact, from that time to the present the harp has been the national symbol of Ireland.

At this point in its evolution the harp was constructed in many shapes and sizes but its general form had basically stabilized into the triangular form we know today. Some of the early European harps were too large to carry, others were very small. Some harps had as few as seven strings: some had up to forty. The harp was held in highest esteem for hundreds of years until the sixteenth century when the lute and keyboard families gained in popularity. The oldest existing harp still extant today is the Brian Boru harp which dates to the eleventh century. Unfortunately many hundreds of harps were destroyed and many harpers killed during the purges foisted onto the Irish by the seventeenth century English Protectorate under Cromwell. Because of this only a few of these old harps have been passed on to us today.

By the eighteenth century many subtle changes were made in the harp, the most notable being the switch from wire strings to gut strings. In part this change was necessary to accommodate the stylistic changes that were occurring in the music at the time. When we study the history of the harp from the vantage point of the twentieth century two distinct types of Celtic harp have evolved: the ancient style and the neoCeltic style. Another style is the large concert pedal harp found in orchestras, but that is beyond the present study. Many contrasting characteristics of the two harp styles will be discussed in the construction section.

The harp described in the following pages has been loosely styled after the Scottish clarseach (harp) commonly called the Queen Mary harp. I have made several changes in the construction and style of this harp without sacrificing the traditional impression of the original. I have tried to simplify the building process and introduce modern building materials which should give the instrument more stability.

I do not recommend that you choose the harp as your first project. It is one of the more complex and exacting of the instruments found in this book and its successful construction requires at least some prior woodworking experience.

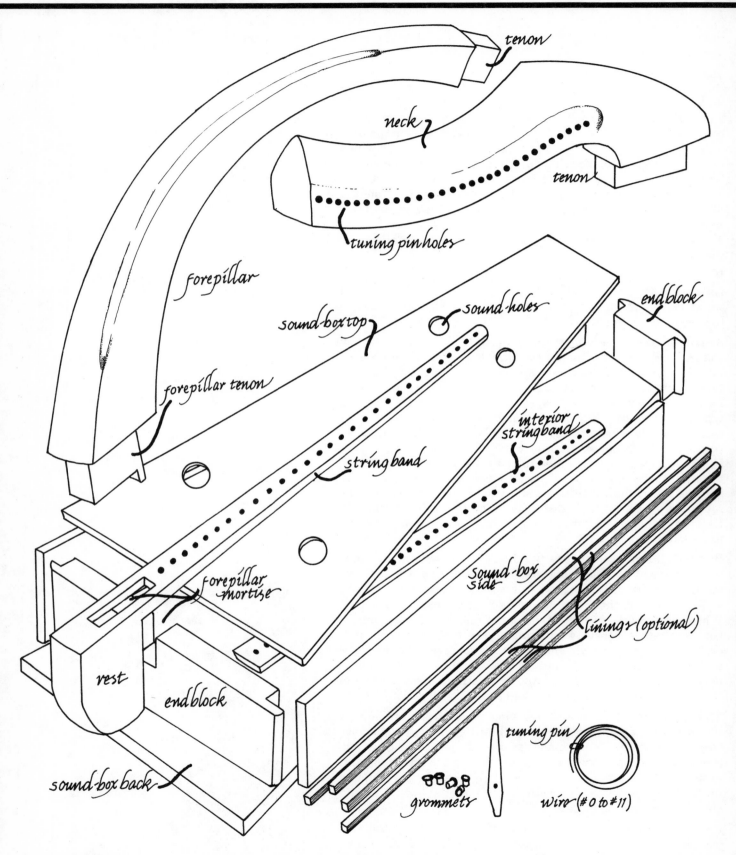

tenon

neck

tenon

tuning pin holes

forepillar

sound box top

sound holes

end block

forepillar tenon

interior stringband

string band

sound-box side

linings (optional)

forepillar mortise

rest

end block

sound-box back

tuning pin

grommets

wire (#0 to #11)

Parts of the Ancient Celtic Harp

MATERIALS
Read instructions carefully before buying materials

Plank of hardwood 1-3/4" x 2" thick, 12" wide, and about 10' long

3/16" to 1/4" sheet of fine plywood approximately 32" x 12" for soundboard

1/4" thick piece of plywood to match the hardwood approximately 32" x 12" for the back

29 machinist taper pins or piano pins or zither pins and tuning wrench

Package of at least 60 brass or silver grommets

Rolls of music wire. Range: #1, #3, #5, #6, #7, #8, #9, #10, #11

ASSEMBLY
Full-size Pattern

1. On a large piece of posterboard or heavy paper make a full-size drawing of the harp. This can be accomplished most easily with an opaque projector or enlarging projector. Tack the posterboard onto the wall and project the image of the harp onto it. By moving the projector backwards or forwards you can create the actual size of the harp on the board. Trace the outline of the projection onto the board. Try the local school or community organization for projectors. If you are unable to find a projector of this sort you may have to transfer measurements from the book to full size. The drawing on page 120 will be your template pattern for the neck and forepillar and will guide you in cutting and adjusting the mortise and tenon joints on the neck, forepillar, and sound-box.

Sound-box

2. The sides of the sound-box may be made from any hardwood material depending on what is available in your area. Maple is excellent, although alder, hornbeam, vermillion, walnut, birch, and Irish willow have been used successfully. Open-grained or relatively unstable woods such as oak and elm are not as appropriate. I chose birch for this sample construction.

Note Ancient Celtic harps differ from the neoCeltic harps in several respects especially in sound-box construction. There are several ways to make sound-boxes. The oldest method is to hollow out a well-seasoned log so that the sides, top, bottom, and soundboard of the harp are made from one piece of wood. The back of the sound-box on these instruments was removable to facilitate stringing and was used by the harpists of old as their combined suitcase and lunchpail as well!

Today the sound-boxes of neoCletic harps are usually built up from separate pieces rather than carved from solid wood. I have chosen to use the built up sound-box in spite of tradition because of the difficulty in obtaining seasoned hardwood logs or thick planks and because a hollowed-out box has a tendency to dry and crack easier than the combination of woods that I suggest here. If, however, you have access to a good dry plank 4" x 32" (or two 2" x 32" pieces glued together) and wish to use the hollowing out technique, drill out whatever possible then clean up the inside recess with a chisel and scraper.

Sides

3. Each side piece measures 26-1/2" x 4" by 3/8" (1). These may be resawn on the band saw or table saw from a larger plank of wood and then sanded smooth.

1 *Side pieces*

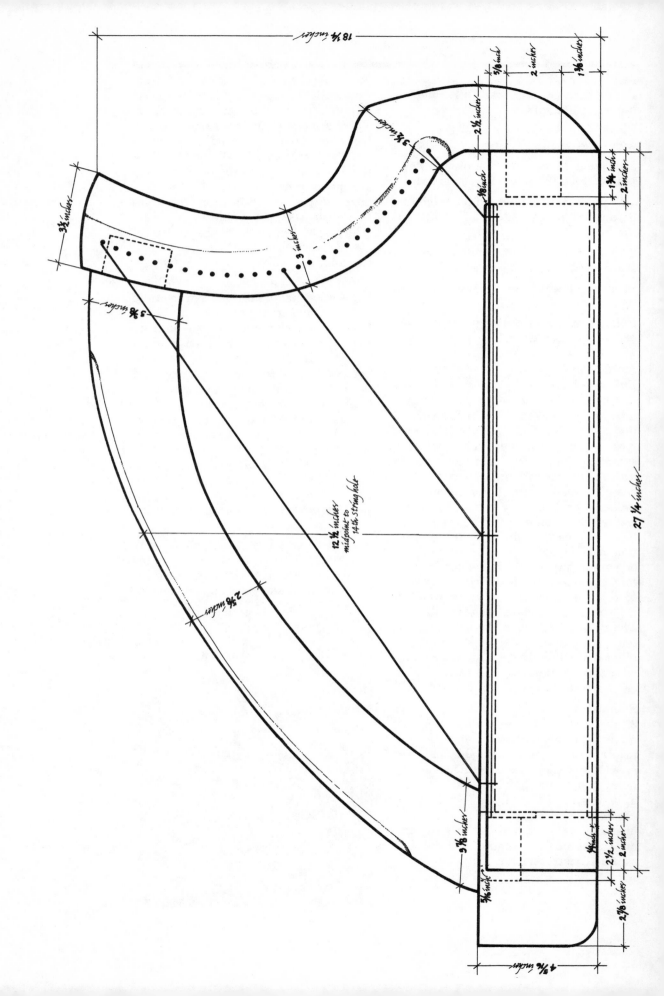

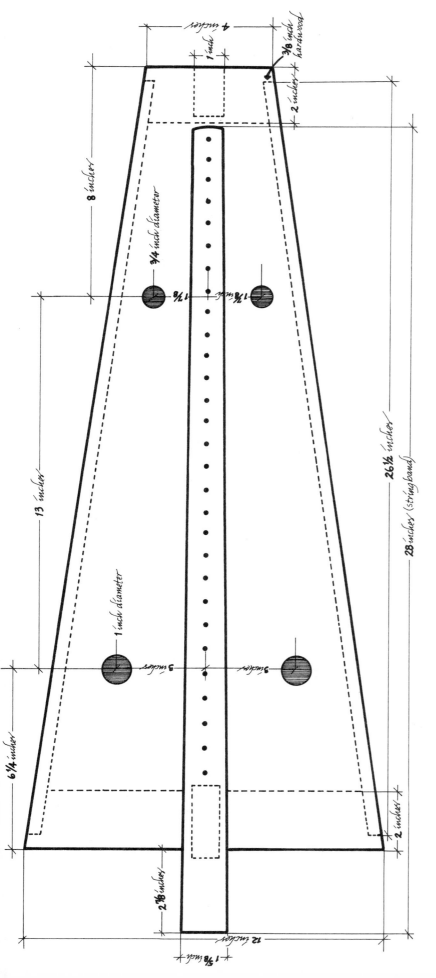

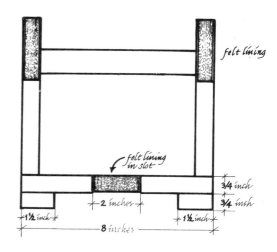

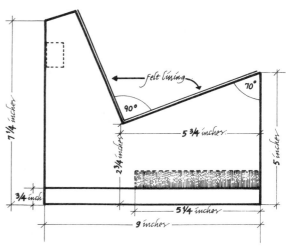

Harp Rest

End Blocks

4. The end blocks are sawn from a 2" thick plank so that the lower end block measures 12" x 4" x 2" and the upper block 4" x 4" x 2" (2). A notch (or rabbet) is now cut along the side edges of each block (A). Set up the end blocks on your bench in their respective positions and balance the sides on them so that you can pencil the configuration of the area to be removed onto each end block. Double check your tracings carefully, then band saw out the notch. Set it up again, making sure that the two end blocks are parallel to each other. Chisel and file the notches for a good fit (3). Apply glue and clamp (4).

Neck and Forepillar

5. Cut the templates from your full-size drawing pattern (see p. 120) and place them on a 1-3/4" thick plank of hardwood (5a, b). Maple, though a bit heavy, is an excellent wood because of its hardness and stability. Pencil the outline onto the wood and cut it out on the band saw. It is important not to cut the tenons to exact size at this point. Leave extra wood around the tenon areas until later (6).

Note The neck and forepillar of most *contemporary* harps are made by building up three layers of wood to the specified dimensions (B).

A

2 *Preparation of end blocks*

3 *Side and end block junction*

4 *Glue and clamp sides to end blocks*

The middle layer is usually maple and slightly wider than the outside pieces which are made from the same material as the sound-box. This keeps the wood colors unified and also confuses the grain patterns thus strengthening the neck and forepillar as a whole unit. This is an optional construction that works well but is not an essential building practice.

6. After rough cutting the neck and forepillar, begin sanding and smoothing some of the ridges and marks that were left by the band saw.

Sound-box/Neck Junction

7. Pencil the outline of the mortise accurately on the top end block of the sound-box (7). Draw the center line first, then arrange the mortise outline as shown (C).

Most of the mortise, which is 1-3/4" deep, may be drilled with a twist bit (8) or 1/2" self-centering bit. Try to drill straight and accurately. Wrap a little masking tape around the drill bit to act as a depth gauge. Next carefully chisel out the remaining wood until you have a clean straight-sided mortise (9).

B

5a *Neck pattern*
5b *Forepillar pattern*

6 *Rough sawn neck and forepillar*

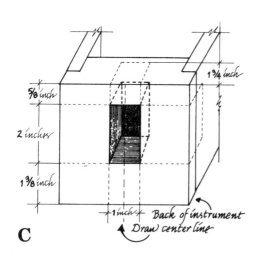

C

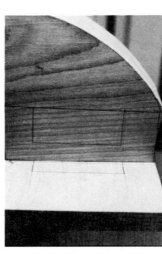

7 *Patterns for neck tenon and end block mortise.*

8 *Drill out mortise*

Neck Tenon

8. Use the neck template to check the position of the neck to the sound-box and make any adjustments necessary to insure a good fit.

9. Draw the neck tenon onto the neck and cut the end to match the depth of the mortise (D) (E). Pencil the outline of the tenon on the neck and double check your measurements as you proceed. The tenon should be cut just slightly larger than the mortise and adjusted later.

A dovetail saw or back saw may be used to cut away excess wood from the neck (10) leaving the tenon which should now be painstakingly fitted to the mortise on the sound-box (11). File, chisel, and sandpaper the components carefully, constantly fitting them until the fit is fairly accurate. Final fitting is done after the forepillar is in place.

Soundboard

10. Ancient harps, since they were hollowed out of a single block of wood, did not have to worry about a separate soundboard. These early sound-boxes were originally carved so that the soundboard was flat. Later, the tension of the strings and some stylistic changes introduced the characteristic "belly" or curve from top to bottom and from side to side. Most soundboards were about 1/4" thick with some variance between the high and low string portions. The disadvantage of this building technique is the shortage of suitable blocks of wood

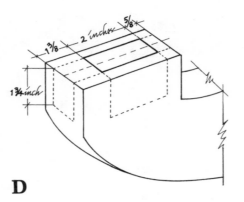

D

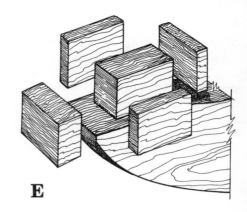

E

9 *End block mortise for neck tenon*

10 *Carefully shape tenon*

and the tendency of the instrument to crack after a period of time. Of course, the instrument can be repaired and if you do have access to this wood you can use this method quite successfully. Another method is to laminate hardwood pieces to get a suitable width. This is more difficult to do and the product is not as strong. For this sample model I have chosen some 3/16" 4-ply aviation plywood because of its strength and because it eliminates having to laminate pieces to achieve the length and width necessary for a separate soundboard. Plywood has reasonable sound qualities and will support the great string tension without too much cracking or distortion.

Note A 1/4" hardwood soundboard may be substituted for both the hollow-box method or the plywood type. Simply cut the soundboard to the shape of the sound-box (12).

String Band

11. A hardwood strip about 1/8" thick and 1-7/8" across at the bottom with a taper to 1" at the top is fashioned in conjunction with the protrusion at the base of the harp. Draw the pattern onto a 1-

3/4" to 2" thick plank of hardwood (maple is again a good choice), cut out the pattern (13) on the band saw, and smooth and true up the surfaces so that they fit the soundboard and the sound-box as shown (14). Glue the string band onto the soundboard using enough clamps or weights to get even pressure all along the length of the soundboard (15).

12. Another reinforcing band, a band matching the approximate dimensions of the first, is now cut and glued to the underside of the soundboard to provide stability against the great string pull that will later be exerted.

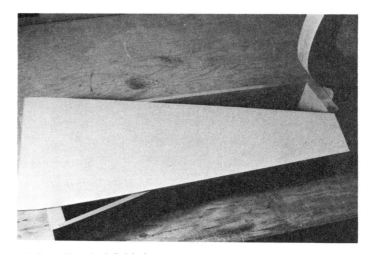

12 *Soundboard of Celtic harp*

11 *Fit neck to sound-box*

13 *String band*

Sound-holes

13. Four sound-holes may now be drilled and sanded (F). The upper holes measure 3/4"; the lower holes are 1". Sound-holes on neoIrish harps are usually placed in the back of the instrument and are oblong and large enough for the hand to enter. This provides access to the interior of the instrument to service the strings. Ancient harps, however, usually had simple holes pierced into the front (or sides) of the instrument and the holes were often surrounded by ornate carving.

Neck Mortise

14. Clamp (no glue yet) the string band/soundboard combination securely onto the sound-box (16). Put the neck onto the sound-box as well. Take your original forepillar pattern (template) and hold it in position to check the alignment and position of the prospective mortises and tenons (17). Draw the mortise pattern accurately onto the underside of the neck where the forepillar will join it and, using the procedure established before, drill and chisel a neat recess into the neck (18).

Mortise at the Base of the String Band

15. Assemble again. Hold the forepillar template in place and check the relative placement of the final mortise at the base of the string band. Draw an accurate outline where the mortise will be cut and proceed to drill and chisel in the same fashion as before (19).

14 *Fit string band to sound-box*

15 *Glue string band to soundboard*

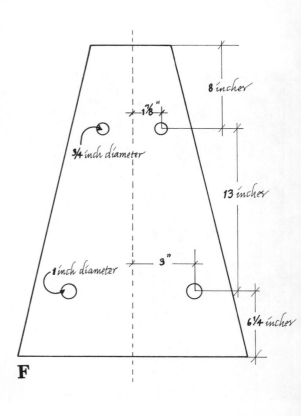

F

Forepillar

16. When you are satisfied that your forepillar template (especially the tenon regions) fits the existing mortise positions in both neck and sound-box, draw it onto the roughed out forepillar itself and painstakingly fashion the tenon on each end to an accurate fit (20a, b). Take enough time to do the job carefully. There is no need to do *all* the fitting at once. True up each part a little at a time and proceed from step to step.

17 *Check fit of forepillar pattern to sound-box and neck*

16 *Fit string band/soundboard onto sound-box*

18 *Neck tenon/forepillar mortise junction*

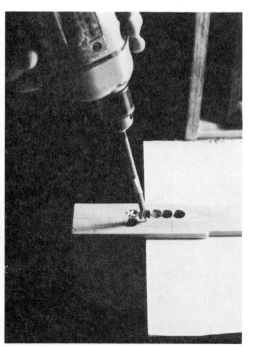

19 *Drill mortise*

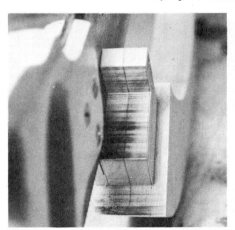

20a *Shape forepillar tenon*

20b *Final tenon shaping*

Shaping

17. With a spokeshave and files, round the shoulder of the neck as shown (21) and bring the remaining curve of the neck to a roof top configuration. This adds to its grace and general appearance. The forepillar traditionally has a structural "T" formation or two-headed reptile carved on the front curve to add ornamentation and stability. To simplify this step however, I have left the forepillar thicker than usual and routered a cove-style groove along most of its length (22) thus visually lightening its bulkiness.

Linings and Back

18. Cut strips of hardwood into 3/8" x 1/4" lengths to fit around the interior of the box thus providing more gluing surface for the soundboard (23). The lining will be perfectly flush with the level of the box on the soundboard side since the soundboard will be glued on top of the box. The back, however, remains removable and will be inset into the back of the sound-box (24). The back must be removable to provide access to the strings as they enter the box through the soundboard. Cut the back from 1/4" plywood and carefully fit it to the back

21 *Shape neck*

22 *Route cove-style groove in forepillar*

23 *Glue and clamp linings on soundboard side*

24 *Glue and clamp recessed lining to hold sound-box back*

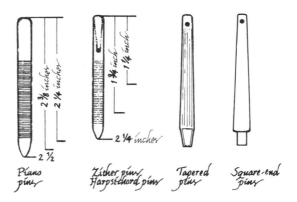

of the box (25). Cut a lining to support the back and glue the lining in the sound-box so that when the back is in place the back of the harp will appear perfectly flat.

Mock-up
19. Mock-up all the components and true any poor joints (26). If you accidently remove too much wood from a mortise/tenon combination, shim any gaps carefully with veneer or bits of the same wood. The better the fit, the longer the harp will remain stable under tension.

Tuning Pins
20. Tapered pins that went completely through the neck were used almost exclusively on the ancient harp. We can approximate this tuning apparatus by buying machinist taper pins (that are 1/4" at the large end) and a matching reamer. The large end of the pin must be ground or filed to fit a zither tuning wrench. These will give service for a long time but are difficult to make because the four facets are *tapered* rather than square. You could also grind a flat configuration of four or two sides and, for tuning, use either a special tuning wrench made by a machinist or a small mechanic's wrench. Clock keys are yet another alternative.

Piano pins or zither pins are used on most neoIrish harps and there is no practical reason why they can't be used on ancient style harps as well. If they are more accessible and you don't mind investing in a piano tuning wrench (or zither wrench) these pins work very well. Piano pins come in different gauge sizes; the most usual sizes are #2, #3, and #4 pins. I suggest using number 2 pins that are 2-1/4" long. The gauge is not critically important as long as you have a drill bit smaller than the pin size. The bit you use in soft hardwoods will have to be smaller than a bit used for very hard woods in order to hold the strings under tension. Be sure to experiment on a scrap piece of wood before putting holes into your harp.

21. The tapered-pin holes may be drilled all the way through the neck with a regular bit, then enlarged to a taper

25 *Sound-box back of Celtic harp*

26 *Mock-up of Celtic harp*

130

(from right to left relative to the player) with the matching reamer. Piano or zither pins do not go through the neck so will be drilled in the left side of the neck relative to the player.

Pin Placement

22. Plot the pin line from the neck template onto the neck (27). Although this is not traditionally done I have hollowed out a recess for the high string pins so that the strings will align a bit more to the vertical. Strings would normally take on a slanting configuration from soundboard to neck as the strings get shorter. NeoIrish harps offset the neck and forepillar to achieve a more vertical alignment. My solution is a centered neck and forepillar like the ancient harps but with a cove fashioned for the upper pins. The cove is optional.

String Holes

23. Plot the string hole arrangement along the string band as shown (G).

I have chosen to use plain metal grommets to reinforce each string hole so that the strings under tension will not cut into the wood so badly. There are other techniques to achieve this purpose but grommets are the simplest. Special harp grommets in varying sizes are also available (see Appendix C).

24. Drill holes into the string band so that the grommets you have procurred fit snugly into them.

Pin Holes

25. Double check your pin placement, then drill holes at the designated points along the neck to receive the pins (28).

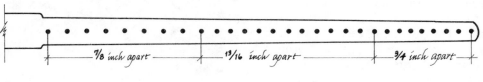

⅞ inch apart — *¹³⁄₁₆ inch apart* — *¾ inch apart*

G

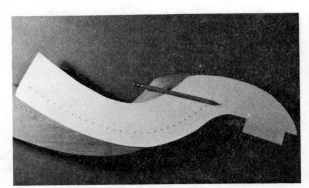

27 *Pin template to mark pin holes on wood*

28 *Drill tuning pin holes.*

Glue Top

27. Position and glue the soundboard to the sound-box. Try to make a good bond with even pressure all around. Heavy rubber bands or rope can be used if clamps are not available. Tacking the soundboard down with short nails is also acceptable.

Last Fitting

28. Proceed with a final adjustment among the three remaining parts, shimming or trimming as required.

Gluing

29. Apply a slow drying glue (Liquid Hide Glue is good for this purpose) to all contact points on the sound-box, forepillar, and neck. Assemble and clamp firmly around the harp with one or two canvas or nylon band clamps (29). Check all joints for alignment. Let dry completely.

Clean-up

30. Clean up glue drips or smears with a chisel, sandpaper, and a damp rag. Trim excess soundboard from around the sound-box and round all edges and corners to give the harp a smooth finish and soft appearance.

Decoration

31. If you desire a decoration it should be done at this point. You can use wood-burning techniques, painting, or carving to enhance the appearance of your harp. Your local library will have books showing some traditional Irish motifs.

Finishing

32. Proceed with sanding stages. (See Finishing Suggestions, Appendix A.) A dark walnut stain is an appropriate pigment to use but this choice depends on your choice of ornamentation. Experiment on a scrap piece of wood first. Apply sealer and/or a final finish of oil, varnish, or lacquer. Polish between coats (30).

Tuning Pins

33. Carefully position the tuning pins along the neck (31). If piano or zither pins are used, leave a few turns for later tightening and tuning of the string.

30 *Staining and finishing for harp*

29 *Use band clamp for gluing components*   31 *Tuning pins with tuning wrench*

Grommets

34. Put grommets along the string band, outside and inside (H).

Music Wire

35. Steel music wire is probably the easiest to find and was used on many early harps. Brass or phosphor bronze are preferred by most makers today. In spite of its relative softness the sound of the brass or bronze string is superior to the steel one. Some experimentation may be necessary depending on which string you choose. I have used steel strings and have distributed the gauges as in diagram (I). Wire strung in this fashion eliminates the need to tie off each string (H).

Tuning Up

36. The harp will tune to approximately a C or D diatonic scale spanning four octaves. Work from the extremes of the string range in towards the middle pulling the strings up to pitch gradually. It is not a good idea to tune the harp up to pitch all at once; rather let it gradually get used to the tension and settle for a day before you tune again (32). Several tunings will be required before it will stabilize. Do this patiently using a piano or pitch pipe to aid you.

37. As the harp is pulled up to pitch check for any movement at the joints. If a particular joint begins to move, release the tension immediately. The neck fore-pillar joint is probably the most susceptible to movement. Ancient harps often have a metal plate or a steel band or two bridging this joint to counteract the great pull of the strings. This may be decorative as well as functional. If necessary, attach the plate on the side opposite the strings.

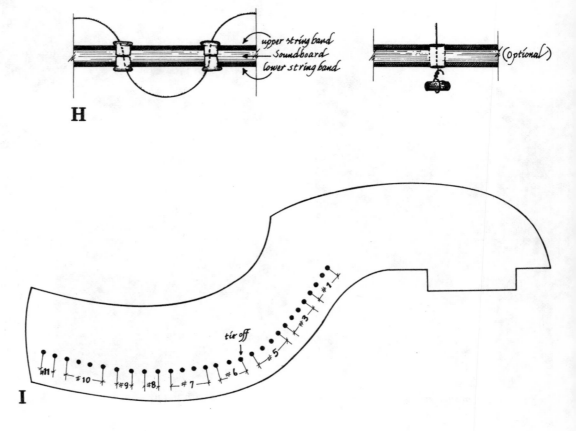

Back

38. Put the back in place (33). If it fits tightly by itself there is no need for further fasteners. If, however, it is loose or rattles, some small screws or other device will be necessary to hold it in place.

PLAYING THE HARP

Pick out chords and melodies by ear and make up your own tunes and compositions. Refer also to the Appendix C for Sylvia Wood's book and by all means subscribe to the Folk Harp Journal (p. 157).

32 *String pattern for harp*

33 *Place back on harp as final step*

The serious luthier will spend as much time on the finishing stages of the instrument as on the actual making. With the development of modern finishing products, however, the length of time can be shortened considerably. Yet now as always the finish will determine the final quality of the instrument.

MATERIALS

There are three or four basic finishes that a beginning craftsman might consider.

Varnish

Traditionally varnish has been the accepted finish for instruments through many ages. It provides a hard surface and offers good protection from the elements. Oil base varnishes were always used for fine violins during the 1700s and although the quality of this finish is certainly unquestionable its extremely long drying time makes its use impractical for the amateur maker. Spirit based varnishes, however, (those that use paint thinner, mineral spirits, or turpentine as a base) provide a good hard protective finish but have a much shorter drying time than oil based varnishes. These varnishes are often designated as interior or furniture varnishes. Spar varnish is not recommended for instruments. Plastic varnishes have recently come onto the market and can be useful for finishing many instruments although their use is not recommended for finer instruments because of the possible dampening effects the plastic may have on the sound quality. It is now possible to purchase water based varnishes. These are easy to use and have the advantage of drying quickly and providing an easy-care surface. Further experiments will determine whether this finish is suitable for musical instruments. Usually two or three light coats of the chosen varnish are sufficient to provide protection for your instrument.

Oil

Another way to finish your instrument is with oil. This is often the finish that is preferred by fine woodworking artists because it seals, conditions, and protects all at once. Danish, linseed, Swedish, and tung oils are a few of the variety of oils available on the market today. Most of these oils are waterproof and most dry to a hard finish which is necessary for instruments. Oils are easy to apply and with a bit of polishing they yield a lustrous finish. Plastic oils are also available but their use for fine musical instruments is limited. Since different oils have different application requirements be sure to follow the directions on the container and talk to a knowledgable person about the different brands available to you. A Swedish oil is a good all purpose oil to begin with. Linseed oil is a traditional finish but requires more work than some of the more contemporary types. Two to four coats of oil are usually sufficient for a good finish on your instrument depending on the hardness of the wood.

Note   Use only *boiled* linseed oil on instruments.

Shellac

Shellac gives an especially fine finish when used with French polishing techniques. Its main detraction, however, is that it is not impervious to liquids. A few drops of water for instance may leave stains on the finish. I find that shellac is most beneficial when used as a sealer applied under varnish. It is a natural product and soaks into the wood and dries hard. Varnish does not have the sealing qualities of shellac but when it is used in conjunction with shellac it yields a strong protective finish. Shellac is usually thinned with methyl hydrate. White shellac is recommended over orange shellac for most purposes.

Lacquer

Lacquer is favored by modern luthiers because it dries quickly and provides a very hard finish. It is usually sprayed on with a compressed or airless spray gun. Brushing is possible but difficult. The beginner may find it easiest to buy lacquer in the compressed can. Though relatively expensive it is the least wasteful method to use and the quickest finish for a short-term project. Several thin coats of lacquer produce a finish that is impervious to almost everything. A sanding sealer is recommended for a sealing coat under the lacquer although this step is not absolutely necessary. Three or four light coats give the best results.

Stains

The application of a stain is optional. Stains are usually used to give the instrument the appearance of warmth and to color the wood to enhance the grain. To stain properly is an art that requires some patience and experimentation. Liquid or gelled ready-to-use stains are the easiest to use. Walnut or mahogany are good basic shades that you might consider. There are also water based, alcohol based, and oil based stains (some of which are called analine dyes) each with its own unique quality. If you require more advice on stains and staining techniques refer to the many good books available on the topic.

FINISHING PROCEDURES
Sanding

1. Sand the instrument with number 120 sandpaper to remove all glue smudges and uneven surfaces as well as to smooth the surface of the wood.

2. Sand again with number 220 sandpaper in order to achieve a perfectly smooth surface. Your fingers can tell when the wood is beginning to be polished.

3. Finer grades of sandpaper may be used for an additional polish although this step is not absolutely necessary.

Stain

4. Stain is optional. Experiment on a scrap of wood before applying the stain to your instrument to see what quality you desire. Follow the directions on the container. If you rub the surface with number 000 steel wool after it has been stained and dried this will lighten or highlight the finish.

Sealing

5. A sealing coat may be applied before or after the stain depending on how dark you want the stain to color. Stain first before sealing for a dark color; seal first and then stain if you want the stain to take lightly. Some stains have sealing elements already in them so you can accomplish two steps at once.

Top Coats

6. After a light rubbing with steel wool (number 000 steel wool) on the stained and sealed surface, dust well with a soft clean rag and find a dust free environment in which to apply the protective coats.

7. Plan ahead the method you will use to apply the top coats. Depending on the finish you choose you may wish to hang the instrument up (spraying the fiddle for instance) or to lay it on a table (varnishing the hammered dulcimer).

8. The first coat should be the lightest or thinned the most (with the exception of oil) and each successive coat that is applied should be slightly heavier.

9. Rub the surface with number 000 steel wool between each coat of finish to remove imperfections and drips and to smooth the surface in preparation for the next coat. Dust well and repeat the application. Very rough spots may be sanded out with a light number 220 sandpaper.

Polish

10. After the last coat of finish has been applied rub the surface lightly with steel wool and polish with a soft cloth to highlight the finish. A higher gloss may be achieved with the use of a pumice or rotten stone polishing aid used with oil or water and buffed to a high shine.

Wax

11. Finally a paste or liquid wax (carnuba wax is good) can be applied to give extra protection and sheen.

Note Most finishes come in high gloss, semi-gloss, matt, or flat types of luster. The choice depends on personal taste. I would suggest that the beginner use a semi-gloss finish because it will not glare as a gloss does yet it will give a nice warm luster that will polish well.

The tools you use to make your instrument *must* be sharp. Dull tools are a source of danger and frustration. With practise and patience you should be able to sharpen your tools so they could shave you. Only then are they ready for working the wood.

Traditionally, sharpening was always done on whet stones using oil or water as a lubricant. The process began with the use of a grinding stone or very coarse stone and progressed to a hard smooth stone. The honing was usually done freehand, allowing experience and feel to guide the blade to produce just the right bevel on the cutting edge. Stones still give a superior cutting edge and the invention of honing guides has made it much easier to get a uniform bevel and shaving edge.

Stones come in a variety of sizes and shapes depending on the size and shape of the blade being sharpened. Some stones are available in combinations, a different grade on each side. A grinding stone is usually necessary to sharpen tools that have been badly damaged or abused or to prepare new blades that are unsharpened. A coarse carborundum stone is often used for blades that have minor chips or are very dull. The India stone, which comes in a medium and fine grit, is an intermediary honing stone used to prepare the blade for a fine stone. A Washita stone is a good basic stone for medium to fine honing as is the soft Arkansas stone. A hard Arkansas stone is usually used to produce a fine shaving edge on the tool and the leather strop to remove the metal burr or wire and put a final polish on the blade. All stones are used with a medium to light grade honing oil. Basically most sharpening jobs require two stones — medium and fine.

Sandpaper and emery cloth have also been used effectively for sharpening. A power sander may be used for the initial grinding stages followed by progressively finer grades of sandpaper and finally a fine emery cloth. It is possible to produce a shaving edge by this method. Sandpaper and emery cloth also have the advantage of being relatively inexpensive and easy to find.

SHARPENING PROCESS

1. The blade may need to be ground on a grinding wheel, belt sander, or coarse stone depending on its condition. Do not leave the blade on a power grinder long enough for it to change color because it will lose its temper and quickly dull again. Cool it in water often as you grind.

2. Hone the blade at a slightly increased angle ($1/2°$ to $1°$) on a medium stone (India, Washita, or soft Arkansas) until an even polished bevel has been achieved across the blade. A honing guide will help you hold a consistent angle and aid in controlling the pressure.

Note The underside of the blade should be flat across its entire width. Lay the blade flat or at a slightly increased angle on its back and grind away until you achieve a flat surface across its width.

3. On a fine stone (hard Arkansas) at the same angle or slightly increased by $1/2°$ hone the blade to a high polish. Take time to do this carefully.

4. To remove the hair edge or burr that will probably develop, pull the blade along a leather strop quickly with good pressure on both sides. This will produce a final polished shaving edge.

Music Wire Conversion Chart

BRITISH GAUGE	AMERICAN GAUGE
00	.0085"
0	.009"
1	.010"
2	.011"
3	.012"
4	.013"
5	.014"
6	.016"
7	.018"
8	.020"
9	.022"
10	.024"

Metric Conversion Chart

Fraction of an inch	mm	Fraction of and inch	mm
1/32	.793	29/32	23.081
1/16	1.587	15/16	23.812
3/32	2.381	31/32	24.606
1/8	3.175	1	25.400
5/32	3.968	1/2 inch	1.27 cm
3/16	4.762	1 inch	2.54 cm
7/32	5.556	1 foot	.30 m
1/4	6.350	1 yard	.91 m
9/32	7.143	.04 inch	1 mm
5/16	7.937	.39 inch	1 cm
11/32	8.731	3.28 feet	1 m
3/8	9.525		
13/32	10.318		
7/16	11.112		
15/32	11.906		
1/2	12.700		
17/32	13.493		
9/16	14.287		
19/32	15.081		
5/8	15.875		
21/32	16.668		
11/16	17.462		
23/32	18.256		
3/4	19.050		
25/32	19.843		
13/16	20.637		
27/32	21.431		
7/8	22.225		

"f"-hole

Renaissance style

Weeping heart

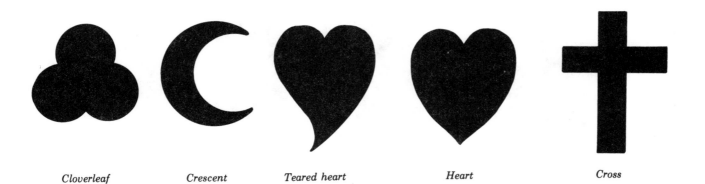

Cloverleaf   *Crescent*   *Teared heart*   *Heart*   *Cross*

Sunset

Navaho Peyote Bird

Starburst

Cloverleaf

Celtic harp

Evening Wisp

Song
Selections

Go Tell Aunt Rhody

This is a traditional play-party song of the Appalachian Mountains which you will find easy to play on the dulcimer with guitar or autoharp accompaniment. It is a simple tune that could be utilized on any instrument designed to play melody. Try playing D minor and G minor chords instead of major chords for variation. Make up your own words.

GO TELL AUNT RHO-DY, GO TELL AUNT RHO-DY, GO TELL AUNT RHO-DY THE

OLD GREY GOOSE IS DEAD.

THE ONE THAT SHE WAS SAVIN' (repeat 3 times)
TO MAKE HER FEATHER BED.

SHE LEFT EIGHT LITTLE GOSLINGS (3x)
TO SCRATCH FOR THEIR OWN BREAD.

THE FOX CAUGHT HER IN THE FIELD (3x)
'FORE SHE COULD FLY AWAY.

THE GANDER IS VERY SAD (3x)
BECAUSE HIS LOVE IS DEAD.

Old Joe Clark

A traditional tune with possibilities of an endless number of verses. I especially enjoy playing this song on the banjo or fiddle. It lends itself well for an extended jam session if played with a variety of instruments. Jug band instruments fit in well to add depth and more rhythm. Make up your own words.

I USED TO LIVE ON A MOUNTAIN TOP, NOW I LIVE IN TOWN. I'M STAYIN' AT THE

BIG HO-TEL COURTIN' BETSY BROWN. FARE THE WELL OLD JOE CLARK, FARE THE WELL I

SAY. FARE THE WELL OLD JOE CLARK, GOOD-BYE BETSY BROWN.

I WISH I LIVED IN ARKANSAS
SITTIN' IN A CHAIR
ONE HAND ON MY WHISKEY JUG
THE OTHER ON MY DEAR.
CHORUS

WISH I HAD A LOVER
I'D PUT HER IN MY TUB
AND THE ONLY TIME I'D LET HER OUT
IS TO FIX ME UP SOME GRUB.
CHORUS

I CLIMBED UP THE MAPLE TREE
AND SHE CLIMBED UP THE GUM,
NEVER SAW A PRETTY GIRL
BUT I LOVED HER SOME.
CHORUS

Shady Grove

Try this melody on the hammered dulcimer by transposing it into E minor. That means each note is simply one note higher than written. This well known American melody is in the Aeolian mode.

NOTE: VERSE MELODY SAME AS CHORUS

WHEN I WAS A LITTLE BOY
I JUST WANTED A KNIFE,
NOW THAT I'M A GREAT BIG BOY
I'M LOOKIN' FOR A WIFE.
CHORUS

CHEEKS AS RED AS THE BLOOMIN' ROSE
EYES OF THE DEEPEST BLUE,
YOU ARE THE DARLIN' OF MY HEART
KNOW THAT I LOVE YOU.
CHORUS

HAD A BANJO MADE OF GOLD
EVERY STRING WOULD SHINE,
THE ONLY SONG THAT I WOULD PLAY WAS
WISH THAT GIRL WAS MINE.
CHORUS

Cripple Creek

This is a good song for any combination of instruments. Don't forget to add some jug band instruments for rhythmic color. Let each instrument take a "break" between verses.

GIRLS ON CRIPPLE CREEK 'BOUT HALF GROWN
JUMP ON A BOY LIKE A DOG ON A BONE.
ROLL MY BRITCHES UP TO MY KNEES,
I WADE OL' CRIPPLE CREEK WHEN I PLEASE.
CHORUS

CRIPPLE CREEK'S WIDE AND CRIPPLE CREEK'S DEEP,
I'LL WADE OL' CRIPPLE CREEK AFORE I SLEEP,
ROADS ARE ROCKY AND THE HILLSIDE'S MUDDY
AND I'M SO DRUNK THAT I CAN'T STAND STEADY.
CHORUS

Will The Circle Be Unbroken

*Written by A. P. Carter, this song has become a bluegrass
classic. It should be quite easy to find a recording for demonstration purposes or to sing along with the melody. The song
sounds especially well with many instruments and voices.*

LORD, I TOLD THE UNDERTAKER,
"UNDERTAKER, PLEASE DRIVE SLOW,
FOR THIS BODY YOU ARE HAULIN',
LORD, I HATE TO SEE HER GO."
CHORUS

I FOLLOWED CLOSE BEHIND HER,
TRIED TO HOLD UP AND BE BRAVE,
BUT I COULD NOT HIDE MY SORROW,
WHEN THEY LAID HER IN THE GRAVE.
CHORUS

Scarborough Fair

*This medieval English riddle song has become popular in the
past few years. Arranged in the Dorian mode this tune has an
especially haunting quality when played on the Appalachian
dulcimer or harp.*

WILL YOU REAP IT WITH SICKLE OF LEATHER?
PARSLEY, SAGE, ROSEMARY, AND THYME.
AND TIE IT ALL UP WITH PEACOCK'S FEATHER
FOR ONCE SHE WAS A TRUE LOVE OF MINE.

WILL YOU PLOUGH IT WITH A LAMB'S HORN?
PARSLEY, SAGE, ROSEMARY, AND THYME.
AND SOW IT ALL OVER WITH ONE PEPPERCORN,
FOR ONCE SHE WAS A TRUE LOVE OF MINE.

WILL YOU FIND ME AN ACRE OF LAND?
PARSLEY, SAGE, ROSEMARY, AND THYME.
BETWEEN THE SEA FOAM AND THE SEA SAND,
FOR ONCE SHE WAS A TRUE LOVE OF MINE.

Camptown Races

A Stephen Foster favorite, this song is suitable for fiddling and foot stomping. Add a banjo, washtub bass, and kazoos for extra entertainment.

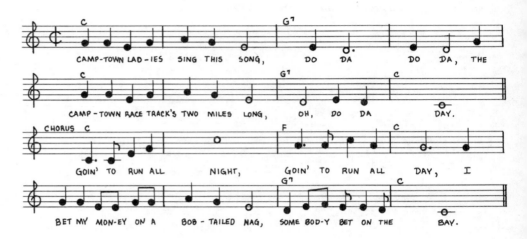

CAMP-TOWN LAD-IES SING THIS SONG, DO DA DO DA, THE
CAMP-TOWN RACE TRACK'S TWO MILES LONG, OH, DO DA DAY.

CHORUS
GOIN' TO RUN ALL NIGHT, GOIN' TO RUN ALL DAY, I
BET MY MON-EY ON A BOB-TAILED NAG, SOME BOD-Y BET ON THE BAY.

OH, THE LONG TAILED FILLY AND THE BIG BLACK HORSE,
DO-DA, DO-DA,
COME TO A MUDHOLE AND THEY ALL CUT ACROSS,
OH, DO-DA-DAY.
CHORUS

I WENT DOWN SOUTH WITH MY HAT CAVED IN,
DO-DA, DO-DA,
I COME BACK NORTH WITH A POCKET FULL OF TIN,
OH, DO-DA-DAY.
CHORUS

Hush Little Baby

Try this simple Texas lullaby on either the Appalachian or hammered dulcimer. Make up your own rhymes.

HUSH, LIT-TLE BA-BY, DON'T SAY A WORD, MA-MA'S GON-NA BUY YOU A MOCK-IN' BIRD.
IF THAT MOCK-IN' BIRD DON'T SING, PA-PA'S GON-NA BUY YOU A DIA-MOND RING.

IF THAT RING IS MADE OF BRASS,
MAMA'S GONNA BUY YOU A LOOKIN' GLASS.

IF THAT LOOKIN' GLASS GETS BROKE,
PAPA'S GONNA BUY YOU A BILLY GOAT.

IF THAT BILLY GOAT DON'T TALK,
MAMA'S GONNA BUY YOU A BIG WHITE HAWK.

IF THAT BIG WHITE HAWK DON'T FLY,
PAPA'S GONNA BUY YOU SOME APPLE PIE.

IF THAT APPLE PIE'S NO GOOD,
MAMA'S GONNA MAKE YOU A LITTLE RED HOOD.

IF THAT LITTLE HOOD FITS RIGHT,
MAYBE YOU'LL SLEEP TIGHT TONIGHT.

Down In The Arkin

*I especially enjoy performing this tune with voice and mouth
bow. I like to give the mouth bow a solo verse now and again.
Banjo, guitar, and some high harmony on the chorus will add
color.*

WELL I HAD A COW THAT SLOB-BER'D BAD DOWN IN THE AR-KAN-SAS. I
TOOK HER TO MY GREAT GRAN-DAD, WAY DOWN IN THE AR-KAN-SAS I
ASKED HIM WHAT TO DO FOR IT DOWN IN THE AR-KAN-SAS, HE
SAID JUST TEACH THAT COW TO SPIT, WAY DOWN IN THE AR-KAN-SAS.

CHORUS
DOWN IN THE AR-KIN, DOWN IN THE AR-KIN, DOWN IN THE AR-KAN-SAS. THE
PRETTI-EST GAL I EV-ER SAW WAS DOWN IN THE AR-KAN-SAS.

I HAD A GAL, HER NAME WAS LIL, DOWN IN THE ARKANSAS.

I HUGGED THAT GAL ALL OVER THEM HILLS, DOWN IN THE ARKANSAS.

HER PA RUN UP AND CALLED ME SON, DOWN IN THE ARKANSAS.

TIED THE KNOT WITH HIS RIFLE GUN, DOWN IN THE ARKANSAS.

CHORUS

HAD A FRIEND, HIS NAME WAS JACK, DOWN IN THE ARKANSAS

HE HAD A HOG NAMED RAZORBACK, ...

FUNNIEST THING YOU EVER HEARD, ...

HE USED THAT HOG TO SHAVE HIS BEARD, ...

CHORUS

She'll Be Comin' Round The Mountain

A good hand-clapping song that is suitable for any combination of instruments. Add your own verses.

SHE'LL BE COM-IN' ROUND THE MOUNTAIN WHEN SHE COMES. SHE'LL BE COM-IN' ROUND THE MOUN-TAIN WHEN SHE COMES. SHE'LL BE COM-IN' ROUND THE MOUN-TAIN, SHE'LL BE COM-IN' ROUND THE MOUN-TAIN, SHE'LL BE COM-IN' ROUND THE MOUN-TAIN WHEN SHE COMES.

SHE'LL BE RIDING SIX WHITE HORSES WHEN SHE COMES. (REPEAT)

OH, WE'LL ALL GO OUT TO SEE HER WHEN SHE COMES. (REPEAT)

OH, WE'LL HAVE A CELEBRATION WHEN SHE COMES. (REPEAT)

Oh, Susanna

A Stephen Foster favorite that sounds most appropriate with a banjo accompaniment.

I COME FROM AL-A-BAM-A WITH A BAN-JO ON MY KNEE. I'M GOIN' TO LOU'-SI-
RAINED ALL NIGHT THE DAY I LEFT, THE WEATH-ER IT WAS DRY. THE SUN SO HOT I

AN-A MY SU-SAN-NA FOR TO SEE. IT
FROZE TO DEATH, SU-SAN-NA FOR TO DON'T YOU CRY.

CHORUS

OH, SU-SAN-NA, OH DON'T YOU CRY FOR ME, FOR I COME FROM AL-A-BAM-A WITH A

BAN-JO ON MY KNEE.

I HAD A DREAM THE OTHER NIGHT,   THE BUCKWHEAT CAKE WAS IN HER MOUTH,
WHEN EVERYTHING WAS STILL.   THE TEAR WAS IN HER EYE.
I THOUGHT I SAW SUSANNA   SAYS I, "I'M COMIN' FROM THE SOUTH,
A-COMIN' DOWN THE HILL.   SUSANNA DON'T YOU CRY."
                                        CHORUS

Pick a Bale of Cotton

The folksinger Leadbelly popularized this southern field holler.
Break this song into leader and response sections. For example,
a leader sings first time through, then everybody responds on
the repeat. Make up your own verses. Many rhythm instruments
will add liveliness.

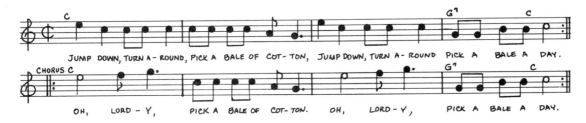

ME AND MY GAL, PICK A BALE OF COTTON.

ME AND MY GAL, PICK A BALE A DAY. (REPEAT)

CHORUS

ME AND MY PA, PICK A BALE OF COTTON.

ME AND MY PA, PICK A BALE A DAY. (REPEAT)

CHORUS

WENT DOWN TO MEMPHIS TO PICK A BALE OF COTTON.

WENT DOWN TO MEMPHIS TO PICK A BALE A DAY. (REPEAT)

CHORUS

The Drunken Sailor

This hornpipe, written in the style of old sailing songs, can
be sung with gusto. Fiddles, drums, and tin whistles would
be most appropriate but a simple leader/verse, response/chorus
arrangement can also be effective.

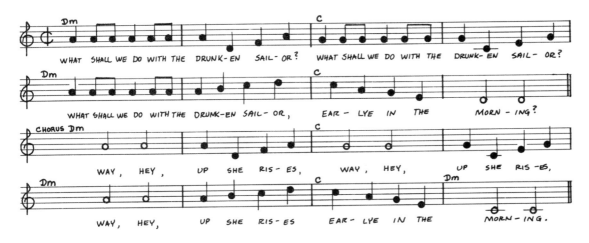

PUT HIM IN THE LONG-BOAT UNTIL HE'S SOBER (3X)

EARLYE IN THE MORNING.

CHORUS

SHAVE HIS BELLY WITH A RUSTY RAZOR (3X)

EARLYE IN THE MORNING.

CHORUS

PUT HIM IN THE SCUPPERS WITH THE HOSE PIPE ON HIM (3X)

EARLYE IN THE MORNING.

CHORUS

Simple Gifts

This is a Shaker hymn and has become a popular melody regardless of what style of music it is used in. Aaron Copland used it in his ballet suite "Appalachian Spring."

'TIS THE GIFT TO BE SIM-PLE, 'TIS THE GIFT TO BE FREE, 'TIS THE GIFT TO COME DOWN WHERE WE OUGHT TO BE, AND WHEN WE FIND OUR-SELVES IN THE PLACE JUST RIGHT, T'WILL BE IN THE VAL-LEY OF LOVE AND DE-LIGHT. WHEN TRUE SIM-PLI-CI-TY IS GAINED, TO BOW AND TO BEND WE WILL NOT BE A-SHAMED. TO TURN, TO TURN-WILL BE OUR DE-LIGHT, AND BY TURN-ING, TURN-ING WE COME 'ROUND RIGHT.

Oh, How Lovely Is The Evening

Try this round with instruments and voices. Start quietly, let the sound gradually build up, then allow it to die away slowly.

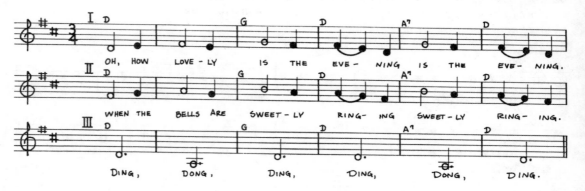

OH, HOW LOVE-LY IS THE EVE-NING IS THE EVE-NING.
WHEN THE BELLS ARE SWEET-LY RING-ING SWEET-LY RING-ING.
DING, DONG, DING, DING, DONG, DING.

Amazing Grace

*This tune is based on an old English melody. The version used
today was written by a white slave owner who turned to religion.
It sounds best with many voices.*

WHEN WE'VE BEEN THERE TEN THOUSAND YEARS,
BRIGHT SHINING AS THE SUN.
WE'VE NO LESS DAYS TO SING GOD'S PRAISE,
THAN WHEN WE FIRST BEGUN.
(REPEAT FIRST VERSE)

WAS GRACE THAT TAUGHT MY HEART TO FEAR,
AND GRACE MY FEAR RELIEVED.
HOW PRECIOUS DID THAT GRACE APPEAR,
THE HOUR I FIRST BELIEVED.
(REPEAT FIRST VERSE)

Cornstalk Fiddle and a Shoestring Bow

*This foot stomping tune really takes on character when accompanied by a fiddle or hammered dulcimer. Add a banjo and
guitar for variety.*

I TUNED UP MY FIDDLE AND I WENT TO A DANCE

I TRIED TO MAKE SOME MUSIC BUT I DIDN'T GET A CHANCE.

CHORUS

I MADE LOTS OF FIDDLES AND MADE LOTS OF BOWS,

BUT I NEVER LEARNED TO FIDDLE LIKE COTTON EYE JOE.

CHORUS

COTTON EYE JOE LIVED 'CROSS THE CREEK.

HE LEARNED TO PLAY THE FIDDLE 'BOUT SEVEN DAYS A WEEK.

CHORUS

Guitar Chords

this sign means
that the two strings
may be played
simultaneously

x this cross means
that the string
should not be
sounded

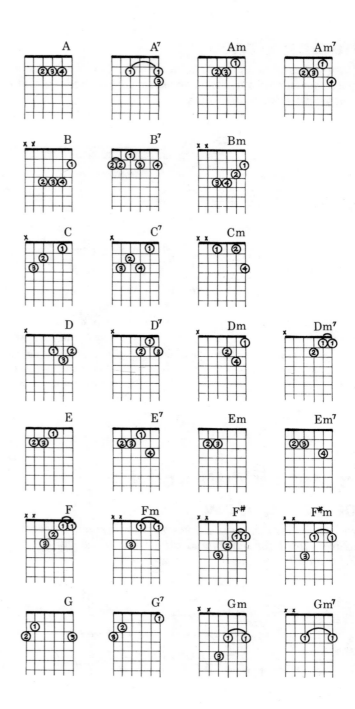

Companies and Suppliers

Albrecht
8635 Yolanda Ave.
Northridge, CA 91324

Atlas West Corp.
20 Jericho Tpke.
Jericho, NY 11753

Belwin Mills
25 Deshon Dr.
Melville, NY 11746

The Brookstone Co.
127 Vose Farm Rd.
Peterborough, NH 03458

Clarus Music
340 Bellevue Ave.
Yonkers, NY 10703

Coastal Abrasive and Tool Co.
1 Nutmeg Dr.
Trumbull, CT 06611

Conover Woodcraft Specialties, Inc.
18124 Madison Rd.
Parkman, OH 44080

Constantine & Son, Inc.
2050 Eastchester Rd.
Bronx, NY 10461

Craft Products Co.
North Ave. and Rte. 83
Elmhurst, IL 60126

Craftsman Wood Service Co.
2727 S. Mary St.
Chicago, IL 60608

Craftswoods
5908C Macleod Tr. S.
Calgary, Alberta Canada T2H OK1

Crane Creek Co.
Box 5553
Madison, WI 53705

Creative Craft Plans
739 Sprague Rd.
Indianapolis, IN 46217

Curtis Woodcraft Supply Co.
344 Grandview ST.
Memphis, TN 38111

The Cutting Edge
3871 Grand New Blvd.
Los Angeles, CA 90066

The Fine Tool Shops, Inc.
20-28 Backus Ave.
Danbury, CT 06810

Frog Tool Co., Ltd.
541 N. Franklin St.
Chicago, IL 60610

Garrett Wade Co., Inc.
302 Fifth Ave.
New York, NY 10001

Gatson Wood Finishes
3630 E. 10th St.
Bloomington, IN 47401

General Woodcraft
100 Blinman St.
New London, CT 06320

GoldblattTool Co.
559-U Osage
Kansas City, KS 66110

International Violin Supply Co.
414 E. Baltimore St.
Baltimore, MD 21202

The Japan Woodworker
1004 Central Ave.
Alameda, CA 94501

John Harra Wood and Supply Co.
39 W. 19th St.
New York, NY 10011

Lee Valley Tools
857 Boyd Ave.
Ottawa, Ontario
Canada K2A 2C9

Leichtung, Inc.
701 Beta Dr., No. 17
Cleveland, OH 44143

Lemont Specialties
Box 271
Lemont, PA 16851

Bill Lewis
3607 W. Broadway
Vancouver, B.C.
Canada V6R 2B8

Love-Built Toys and Crafts
2907 Lake Forest Rd.
Tahoe City, CA 95730

Marina Music
1892 Union St.
San Francisco, CA 94123

Mason & SullivanCo.
39 Blossom Ave.
Osterville, MA 02655

Masonry Specialty Co.
172 Westbrook Rd.
New Kensington, PA 15068

Merritt Abrasive Products, Inc.
201 W. Manville
Compton, CA 90224

Frank Mittermeier, Inc.
3577 E. Tremont Ave.
Bronx, NY 10465

National Artcraft Supply Co.
23456 Mercantile Rd.
Beachwood, OH 44122

Frank Paxton Lumber Co.
6311 St. John Ave.
Kansas City, MO 64123

Sculpture House, Inc.,
38 E. 30th St.
New York, NY 10016

Shopsmith, Inc.
750 Center Dr.
Vandalia, OH 45377

U.S. General Supply Co.
100 General Pl.
Jericho, NY 11753

Vitali Import Co.
5944 Atlantic Blvd.
Maywood, CA 90270

Joseph F. Wallo
1319 F St. N.W.
Washington, DC 20004

H.L. Wild
510 E. 11th St
New York, NY 10009

Wood Carvers Supply Co.
3056 Excelsior Blvd.
Minneapolis, MN 55416

Woodcraft Supply Corp.
313 Montvale Ave.
Woburn, MA 01801

The Woodworkers Store
21801 Industrial Blvd.
rogers, MN 55374

Woodworkers Supply
11200 Menaul N.E.
Alburquerque, NM 87112

Periodicals

Banjo Newsletter
1301 Hawkins Ln.
Annapolis, MD 21401

Dulcimer Players News
RFD 2, Box 132
Bangor, ME 04401

Mandolin Notebook
12704 Barbara Rd.
Silver Spring, MD 20906

Mugwumps Instrument Herald
12704 Barbara Rd.
Silver Spring, MD 20906

Fine Woodworking
Box 355
Newtown, CT 06470

Pickin'
401 N. Broad St.
Philadelphia, PA 19108

Sing Out!
270 Lafayette St.
New York, NY 10012

Canada Folk' Bulletin
101-337 Carrall St.
Vancouver, B.C., Canada V6B 2J4

Folk Harp Journal, Box 161
Mount Laguna, CA 92048

Autoharp A chording zither invented in the late eighteenth century that has a simplified damping mechanism permitting a person to play chords by depressing buttons.

Back saw A fine-toothed rectangular saw that has extra reinforcing along the back of the blade. Used for fine cuts.

Bag pipes A reed instrument characterized by a bellows-blown or mouth-blown air reservoir. It has a fingered melody pipe (chanter) and drone pipes.

Ball-end string A small metal reinforcement placed in the loop of a string to help support the pull on the hitch pins.

Band saw An electric saw characterized by a continuous thin blade in the form of a loop.

Banjo A plucked chordophone of African origin popularized in the United States during the nineteenth century.

Balalaika A Russian chordophone of the guitar family. It has a triangular shape with four strings.

Bass bar A long narrow piece of softwood glued into many bowed instruments to help transfer vibrations and reinforce the soundboard.

Blowing Air pressure caused by lungs and muscles.

Bodhran Literally "to deafen." A hand-held single skin drum used primarily in Irish music.

Bottleneck A glass or metal "noter" (sometimes broken neck from bottle) used to slide along strings for special effect.

Bowing A sound production technique for stringed instruments which utilizes coarse hair under tension.

Brace and bit A boring tool having a crank (brace) which holds a drill or auger (bit).

Bridge A piece of wood or metal that helps transmit vibrations to the sound-box on stringed instruments. Also delineates a specific string length.

Center brace A support glued in the middle of some stringed instruments to help stabilize the back and sides.

Chamfer To cut away the edge of a board.

Chimes A family of metal percussion instruments.

Chordophone A musical instrument having strings as tone-producing elements.

Cimbalom A hammered zither (dulcimer) from Hungarian gypsy origin. It has two bridges and three courses of strings.

Clarseach The Scottish name for the ancient Irish harp.

Clock key Sometimes used for turning tuning pins on stringed instruments.

Concentric waves Ever enlarging circles all having the same center.

Concert pitch A standard pitch by which European and North American musicians gauge their tuning.

Coping saw A saw with a narrow blade set in an open frame used to cut curves.

Cure To age or dry wood.

Diatonic scale A standard scale of eight notes to the octave with no chromatic intervals.

Dominant pitch The fifth scale degree of a scale.

Dovetail saw A small fine-toothed back saw for small accurate cuts.

Dremel tool A small hobbist's router.

Drum Any instrument that is beaten for its primary effect. Usually a skin or membrane stretched over a resonator.

Dulcimer (dulcimore) A fretted zither deriving from the Appalachian Mountain region in the United States.

End block A block of wood usually found at the end of the sound-box which stabilizes the top, sides, and back.

English horn Similar to but larger than an oboe.

Epinette des Vosages The name for the French fretted dulcimer.

Equidistant Being an equal distance from two or more points.

Fiddle Alternative name for a violin played in a folk or country style.

Fifth scale degree The dominant scale degree or note with the most harmonic significance besides the first scale degree.

File A steel tool with a rough face for smoothing or removing wood or metal.

Fingerboard The area of a stringed instrument along which notes are stopped with the fingers.

Fitting an instrument Putting the strings and other final details on an instrument in preparation for playing.

Flue hole The sound production hole found in recorder type instruments.

Flute A ubiquitous wind instrument usually tubular with a varying number of holes and keys.

Frailing style A banjo picking style.

Fret The metal ridges on stringed instruments that help delineate notes.

Fretboard See Fingerboard.

Fretless banjo An early or backwoods style of banjo without frets on its fingerboard.

Fret saw A fine-bladed saw with a deep open frame used to cut small curves and scroll work. Also a saw used to cut fret slots.

Fretwire Small metal bars arranged across the fingerboard of many stringed instruments delineating a specific scale.

Friction pegs   Violin style pegs conically shaped to fit tightly in a hole.

Froe   A woodworking tool used to split segments of logs.

Forepillar   The supporting member of a harp found opposite the sound-box.

Glissando   A fast pattern or sweep of notes. Sliding up and down a scale.

Glockenspiel   A percussion instrument characterized by tuned metal bars.

Gourd   Any number of fleshy fruits with hard shells.

Gourd bow   A musical bow with a gourd attached as a resonator.

Grain configuration   The pattern of wood grain found in a board which yields useful information for the woodworker.

Grommet   A metal eyelet or ring used to reinforce holes.

Ground bow   Aboriginal stringed instrument found in New Guinea and Africa which uses a pit in the ground as a resonator.

Guitar tuner   String tensioning devices found on guitars.

Gut bucket   Washtub bass.

Gut string   Music string made from the sinew of animals.

Hack saw   A fine-toothed saw with an open frame specifically designed to cut metal.

Hammered dulcimer   Multi-stringed zither played with mallets.

Hand twist drill   Hand drill for making small holes with a twist bit.

Hardwood   Wood derived from deciduous or leafy (not evergreen) trees.

Harp   An ancient chordophone with strings that run more or less perpendicular to the plane of the sound-box.

Harpsichord   A stringed keyboard instrument with plucked strings. Forerunner to the piano, it originated in the sixteenth century.

Heel   The stablized end of the fingerboard of a stringed instrument (as in the guitar) which is attached to the sound-box.

Hitch pin   A small pin which anchors the end of a taut string. The other end is usually attached to a tuning mechanism.

Hone   To sharpen on a stone or other fine abrasive material.

Hummle   The German ancestor to the Appalachian Mountain dulcimer.

Humle   Folk zither of Denmark.

Ionian mode   A major diatonic scale in the modal system of tuning first evolved by the Greeks.

Jigsaw   Tool designed to cut ornate or curved patterns and designs in relatively thin pieces of wood.

Jointer Tool designed to smooth and level medium sized lengths of wood.

Jug band Musical group characterized by use of home implements for instruments.

Kalimba African thumb piano. Sansa.

Keyhole saw A long pointed hand saw used to cut interior holes.

Key note The first scale degree or "home base" note. Tonic note.

Koto A long Japanese zither with thirteen silk strings and moveable bridges.

Langesleik Ancient folk zither of Norway.

Langspil Bowed zither of Iceland.

Lumberjack piano A hammered dulcimer.

Lute A large family of chordophones dating back to 2,000 B.C. Characterized by a fretted neck and oval sound-box.

Luthier Literally, a lute maker. Generally, a maker of fine musical instruments.

Lyre Chordophone with strings attached to a yoke that lie in the same plane as the resonator. Characterized by two arms and a crossbar.

Machine tuner A geared tuning device found on many stringed instruments (especially guitar).

Mallets Percussion sticks used for striking strings, drums, and other percussion instruments.

Melody string The string closest to the player on an Appalachian Mountain dulcimer on which the melody is noted.

Membrane The skin or vibrating cover on a drum.

Minor scale A diatonic scale with the third note (and sometimes sixth and seventh notes) lowered a half step.

Modal A system of scales evolved by the Greeks which gave each scale a particular tonality or feeling.

Mortise A hollowed out space in a piece of wood into which a corresponding projection fits forming a joint.

Mosquito drum A form of ground bow found in Haiti.

Mouth bow Ancient single-stringed instrument consisting of a string and bowed branch which uses the mouth as a resonating chamber.

Neck The instrument member along which stringed instruments are usually noted.

Nodal point A point on a vibrating object (string or bar) where the least vibration takes place.

Noise A subjective term. That sound which is often undesirable or too abstract to determine a specific pitch.

Noter A stick or dowel held in the left hand to facilitate a melody. Used instead of the fingers.

Nut A small piece of hardwood that runs at right angles to the strings to help delineate the string length of an instrument.

Oboe Double reed wind instrument.

Octave A span of eight notes. Each octave doubles (or halves) the number of vibrations per second.

Peg head The end of a stringed instrument to which the tuning mechanisms are attached.

Perfect fifth (sol-do) A significant and strong harmonic interval in Western music.

Piano A stringed keyboard instrument with hammered strings.

Piano wrench A key used in tuning piano strings.

Pick A flexible plectra used to enhance the sound of plucked strings.

Pinblock A piece of extra hard wood in which tuning pins are seated.

Pit harp See *ground bow*.

Pitch The subjective term for vibrations per second.

Pitch pipe Tuning mechanism which gives a standard pitch.

Plectrum A flexible pick used for plucking strings.

Pot A resonating chamber on a banjo.

Psaltery A plucked zither known from Medieval times on.

Psanterim An early form of hammered dulcimer.

Radial arm saw An electric saw used primarily for cross cutting wood.

Rat-tail file A round conical file.

Rasp A coarse file.

Reamer A tool with sharp edges for enlarging or tapering a hole.

Rebec A bowed stringed instrument of Middle Ages and Renaissance times.

Recorder An end-blown instrument with a conical bore, built in several sizes. Used extensively during Renaissance and Baroque times.

Resaw To saw wood planks into thinner slabs. Cutting wood on edge.

Resonator A hollow air-filled cavity on instruments which helps amplify the sound.

Rhythm A regular repetition of sound, beat, or movement.

Router A tool which removes or digs out grooves or small areas of wood.

Saddle Part of the bridge mechanism on a guitar.

Santir A dulcimer of the Arabs and Persians with a trapezoid sound-box and played with light mallets.

Scale Any fixed set of tones having certain intervals between them.

Scheitholt A folk zither of Germany, considered by many to be an early ancestor to the Appalachian Mountain dulcimer.

Scroll An expanding spiral found at the head of some stringed instruments.

Skill saw A portable electric carpenter's saw with a circular blade.

Skiptooth blade A blade with extra spacing between the teeth for sawing hard-to-cut materials.

Sound Audible waves caused by movement or vibration of an object.

Soundboard That part of an instrument most responsible for increasing the vibrating area thus amplifying the sound.

Sound-box An enclosed body of air which reinforces and amplifies the sound of an instrument.

Sound-chamber See *sound-box*.

Sound-hole A decorative and functional hole in the sound-box which helps let sound out of the box. The edges of the holes also vibrate giving more character to the tone.

Soundpost A softwood post set in some bowed instruments to transfer vibrations between the top and back. Also helps support the pressure of the strings on the soundboard.

Sound waves A sequence of compressions and rarefactions caused by molecular movement of the air which in turn is caused by a vibrating object.

Spike fiddle Folk fiddle characterized by a stick (neck) pierced through a hollow container with one or more bowed strings.

Spokeshave A type of hand plane with handles on both sides useful for planing curved surfaces.

Striking To tap, beat, hammer, or hit.

String band A reinforcing strip for the strings found down the center of the soundboard in a harp.

Strum A rapid movement of the hand across the strings of an instrument.

Strum hollow A "decoupling" area on an Appalachian Mountain dulcimer where picking and strumming are usually done.

Syncopation An "offbeat" rhythm. A rhythm that reinforces the weak beats in a measure of time.

Tabla An East Indian drum.

Table saw An electric woodworking saw especially designed to cut lengths of lumber (rip cut).

Tailpiece A piece of hardwood opposite the tuning pegs to which the strings of an instrument are anchored.

Taut Tight but not too tight.

Template A cut-out pattern used for design transfer.

Tenon A tongue of wood cut so that it will fit into a hole of another piece forming a joint.

Timbre Tone quality.

Tine of a fret That portion of a fret that fits tightly into a fine slot cut on the fingerboard thus holding it in place.

Toggles A crosspiece attached to a rope or string to help tighten a drumhead.

Tone A vocal or musical sound. A sound quality.

Tongue The vibratory element in certain percussion instruments such as the kalimba and tongue drum.

Tonic note The "home base" or first step of a scale in the European system of music. Many folk tunes begin and end on this note.

Trapezoid A figure with four sides, two of which are parallel.

Treble bridge The bridge over which the higher pitched strings cross the left hand bridge (relating to the hammered dulcimer).

Trombone A brass wind instrument with a telescopic slide for pitch variation.

Trumpet A lip-vibrated wind instrument made from a variety of materials. Usually has three valves today.

Tuner A mechanism by which the pitch of a string can be changed.

Tuning pin A pin designed to be turned by an accompanying wrench to loosen and tighten strings on an instrument.

Tuning wrench A device used to grip a tuning pin in socket fashion.

Veneer Very thin slabs of wood.

Vibration A to and fro movement of an object. Those that occur at a rate of 20 to 20,000 times a second are usually audible.

Violin A four-stringed bowed instrument that reached its evolutionary peak during the sixteenth and seventeenth centuries in Italy and is still used extensively today.

Vise A mechanical holding device.

Waisted guitar Describes the shape of the sound-box of a guitar.

Washtub bass A single-stringed folk instrument used to simulate the bass line of a tune.

Whetstone A very hard stone used for sharpening metal blades.

Xylophone A percussion instrument comprised of a series of graduated tuned wooden slabs laid parallel to each other.

Zither Any stringed instrument which has strings stretched from end to end or side to side.

Zither pins Tuning pins of a certain size and shape designed for use on zithers.